ROWMAN & LITTLEFIELD PUBLISHERS, INC.

Published in the United States of America
by Rowman & Littlefield Publishers, Inc.
4720 Boston Way, Lanham, Maryland 20706

12 Hid's Copse Road
Cumnor Hill, Oxford OX2 9JJ, England

Copyright © 1998 by Rowman & Littlefield Publishers, Inc.

British Library Cataloguing in Publication Information Available

Library of Congress Cataloging-in-Publication Data

Ferber, Abby L., 1966–
    White man falling : race, gender, and white supremacy / Abby L.
Ferber.
        p.   cm.
    Includes bibliographical references and index.
    ISBN 0-8476-9027-X (hardcover : alk. paper).
    1. White supremacy movements—History—United States—20th
century.   2. Whites—United States—Race identity.   3. Racism—
United States—History—20th century.   4. Sexism—United States—
History—20th century.   5. Miscegenation—United States.   6. United
States—Race relations.   7. Discourse analysis—Social aspects—
United States.   I. Title.
E184.A1F46   1998
305.8'00973—dc21   98-22813
                                                        CIP

Design by Lori Schlosser

Printed in the United States of America

∞ ™ The paper used in this publication meets the minimum requirements of
American National Standard for Information Sciences—Permanence of Paper for
Printed Library Materials, ANSI Z39.48—1984.

WHITE MAN FALLING

Race, Gender, and White Supremacy

Abby L. Ferber

ROWMAN & LITTLEFIELD PUBLISHERS, INC.
Lanham • Boulder • New York • Oxford

WHITE
MAN
FALLING

For Sydney

CONTENTS

ILLUSTRATIONS

ACKNOWLEDGMENTS

Research for this book has been supported by various grants, including a research support grant from the Center for the Study of Women in Society and a graduate fellowship award from the Humanities Center, both at the University of Oregon; a Committee on Research and Creative Works grant from the University of Colorado at Colorado Springs; and an American Sociological Association/National Science Foundation Fund for the Advancement of the Discipline Award.

I am thankful to the faculty and staff of the Sociology Department at the University of Oregon, where I began this research as a graduate student, and at the University of Colorado at Colorado Springs, where I completed this work. Both departments have provided a supportive and nurturing environment that made conducting this research easier.

I would like to express my sincere appreciation to Sandra Morgen, Linda Fuller, Miriam Johnson, Forest Pyle, John Lie, Ken Liberman, Stanley Aronowitz, and Steven Seidman, for their critical insight at various stages throughout this project, as well as the helpful feedback of various anonymous reviewers. I would like to thank others who have provided suggestions regarding specific pieces of the manuscript or simply offered encouragement at various points throughout this project: Dorothea Olkowski, Charles Gallagher, David Theo Goldberg, Patricia Hill Collins, Elizabeth Higginbotham, Kathleen Blee, and Tim Bartlett. I am grateful to my friends Debbie Storrs and Tugrul Ilter, whose conversations and informal mentoring have proven invaluable.

I am especially appreciative of the terrific staff at Rowman & Littlefield, who sped this book to publication. I would like to thank Dean Birkenkamp for both his editorial expertise and his encouragement, as well as editorial assistant Rebecca Hoogs, production editor Lynn Gemmell, and copy editor Luann Reed-Siegel.

I would like to thank the various organizations, and their dedicated staff, who work tirelessly to monitor and combat the far right, and whose work and expertise have been invaluable to me, especially the Anti-Defamation League, the Coalition for Human Dignity, the Northwest Coalition against Malicious Harassment, Political Research Associates, and the Southern Poverty Law Center. I would especially like to thank Chip Berlet, Jean Hardisty, Mark Potok, Eric Ward, Bill Wassmuth, and Leonard Zeskind. I am also grateful to Emory Smith for sharing his collection of *NSV Reports* with me. And I could not have undertaken this research without the special collections department of the Knight Library at the University of Oregon and their helpful staff. I would especially like to acknowledge assistance provided by Will Harmon.

I want to express my sincere gratitude to my *entire* family, who have always shown great enthusiasm and interest in my work. I am especially grateful to my parents, Gary Ferber (1937–1990) and Shelly Ferber Plasco, who taught me to value the pursuit of knowledge and justice. Most importantly, I am grateful to Joel Pollack, not only for contributing to this project at every stage in myriad ways, but for his love, support, and respect.

The following have been reprinted, in part or whole, with or without revision, with permission.

Ferber, Abby L. 1995. Exploring the social construction of race: Social science research and the study of interracial relationships. In *American mixed race: The culture of microdiversity*, edited by Naomi Zack. Lanham, Md.: Rowman & Littlefield.

———. 1995. "Shame of white men": Interracial sexuality and the construction of white masculinity in contemporary white supremacist discourse. *Masculinities* 3, no. 2 (Summer):1–24.

———. 1997. Of Mongrels and Jews: The deconstruction of racialised identities in white supremacist discourse. *Social Identities* 3, no. 2 (April):193–208.

———. 1998. Deconstructing whiteness: The intersections of race and gender in U.S. white supremacist discourse. *Ethnic and Racial Studies* 21, no. 1 (January):48–63 (Ethnic and Racial Studies, Department of Sociology, University of Surrey, Guilford, Surrey GU2 5XH).

———. 1998. White supremacist movement in the U.S. today. In *Race and ethnic conflict*, edited by Fred L. Pincus and Howard J. Ehrlich, second edition. Boulder, Colo.: Westview Press.

The following illustrations have been reprinted with permission.

Figures 1a and 1b: Recruiting women and families (*The Spotlight*, 20 January 1986, 16). [Liberty Lobby, Inc., 300 Independence Avenue S.E., Washington, D.C. 20003.]

Figure 4: Fruits of mythical racial equality (*The Thunderbolt*, September 1981, 3); Figure 5: ERA leads to interracial sexuality (*The Thunderbolt*, February 1980, 12); Figure 8: Jewish brain power (*The Thunderbolt*, June 1975, 8).

Figure 6: Endangered species (*White Power*, December 1980, 9); Figure 10: Only the stormtrooper can stop this (*White Power*, September 1973, 6); Figure 11: Endangered species? (*White Power*, no. 101, 1); Figure 12: Mother and child (*White Power*, no. 101, 3.)

PART I

CONSTRUCTING RACE AND GENDER

1

THE BOUNDS OF WHITENESS

There is a double standard for hatred, as there is for so much else. . . . We are not allowed to hate. They are. . . . Every oppressed people worth its salt hates its oppressors. We should feel no more guilty about hating our enemies than a rodent should feel about hating a snake. . . . Enmity is a key component of the art of individual and group survival. The man who hates to hate is only half a man and a poor defender of his family and race. . . . Without love there is no creation. Without hate the creation cannot be defended. Hate is just as much a unifier as love.[1]

For the writers and readers of *Instauration*, an overtly racist and anti-Semitic white supremacist journal, hatred is an integral part of life. It is every man's duty to defend his own kind against his enemies: in this case, Jews, African Americans, and all nonwhites. And as this passage suggests, hatred is essential to protecting the race. In sharp contrast to the increasingly subtle deployment of racist codifications that pervade mainstream discourse, white supremacist hatred is blatant.

Throughout white supremacist discourse, whites are depicted as the victims of racial oppression. Another article asks,

How much damage does minority racism do as it requires the Majority to keep its mouselike feet on the treadmill; fork over a disproportionate share of the taxes; or battle in the overseas wars? . . . daily, at all hours, the minority racist makes his appearance, alternately complaining, accusing, plotting, sleuthing, whining, gloating, demanding, inserting and twisting his ideological dagger, as he attacks the majority in a thousand different ways.[2]

Inverting the reality of racial oppression, thousands of articles in dozens of different white supremacist publications paint an overwhelming picture of the white race under attack.

White supremacist discourse is strange to read for many reasons, but one of the most obvious is its overt focus on whiteness. We are not used to thinking about whiteness when we think about race. Books and courses on race usually focus on the experiences of racial minority groups, the victims of racism. And this is the logic driving the white supremacist emphasis on whiteness: whites are now the victims of racism. I too want to take up this focus on whiteness, but for very different reasons. Race, I argue, shapes the lives of everyone, victims and oppressors. And, while I strongly disagree with the notion that whites are now the victims of racism, I want to encourage an interrogation of whiteness.

Since race is believed to be something that shapes the lives of people of color, whites often fail to recognize the ways in which their own lives are shaped by race. Recent scholarship argues that we need to extend our analyses to explore white identity and privilege.[3] As Toni Morrison maintains, we need to examine "the impact of racism on those who perpetuate it."[4]

Not only do traditional conceptions of race exclude the experiences of whites, they also prevent us from understanding racial *privilege*, relieving whites of responsibility for racism. "Racism, from this perspective, disadvantages others, but is not shown to advantage whites."[5] Oppression and privilege, however, are tied together. And as recent studies demonstrate, white identity developed historically as a consolidation of privilege.[6]

Focusing on the victims of racism, sociologists have failed to explore the way race shapes the lives of white people, often viewing the experiences of whites as raceless and, therefore, the norm. Embarking on a new course, Morrison asserts that white American identity is constructed through its relationship with and representation of an African Other, created in opposition to this Africanist presence. Recently, sociologists and other scholars have begun to take a similar approach, systematically exploring the construction of white racial identity.[7]

This book contributes to the growing body of research on racism and the construction of whiteness. The central project of the contemporary white supremacist movement is the articulation of a white, male identity. I believe that exploring this process contributes not only to our understanding of the white supremacist movement, but also to the larger process of the construction of racialized identities. Since the movement defines whiteness in highly gendered terms, such a study also sheds light on the interconnectedness of race and gender.

Exploring white supremacist discourse has been personally relevant in ways I did not expect. This research has highlighted the contradictions within my own racial identity. I am a white Jewish woman. I am privileged as a white person and usually viewed by others as white. Taking my whiteness for granted, reading white supremacist discourse was at times shocking. I am reminded that my ancestors were not considered white and that some people still do not consider me to be white—contemporary white supremacists define Jews as nonwhite, the antithesis of whiteness, a distinct race that must be eliminated. I found studying white supremacy to be a curious experience, a personal encounter with the construction of race. Reading white supremacist discourse is like moving between two worlds, one where I am privileged, another where I am despised and attacked; one where I am white, another where I am the nonwhite seed of Satan; one where I am safe and privileged, one where I am always feared and marked for death.

Whether or not I define myself as Jewish, I am constantly defined by others as Jewish. What does this mean? What exactly is Jewishness? It is not simply a religious designation one may choose, as I once naively assumed. I have been told by colleagues, however, that Jews are not a race, and should not be included in classes about race. Through my research, Jewishness has become both clearer and more ambiguous. The questions I have encountered in thinking about Jewish identity highlight the central issues involved in studying race today. Race is a social category, constructed in different times and places for different political purposes. There is no simple answer to the question of whether or not Jews are a race, because what is and is not a racial designation, and who is included within various racial classifications, is unstable and changes over time.

Perhaps my interest in dissecting my own racial identity has driven my interest in exploring the meaning and construction of whiteness today. In white supremacist discourse, whiteness is elaborated and defended because it is perceived to be threatened, and it is this threat that interests me. What took me most by surprise, however, was the way in which this threat was almost exclusively articulated as the threat of interracial sexuality. It is an understatement to claim that white supremacy is obsessed with interracial sexuality. A recurring theme, it serves as a powerful and enduring metaphor for the danger of transgressing racial and gender boundaries. Poststructuralist theory has revealed the centrality of borders to the construction of coherent identities. Far more than a lurid preoccupation, the obsession with interracial sexuality is part of the process of boundary maintenance essential to the construction of race and gender identity.

While sociology usually proceeds with the assumption that there is a reality that exists independent of texts and defines texts as mere representations of that reality, there is also a strong sociological tradition that argues that reality is a social construct.[8] In other words, what we know about the world and ourselves—about reality—is shaped by our culture and social interaction. We understand and make sense of the world through ideology. We have no access to the material realm except through textual narratives, stories we tell ourselves in order to make sense of the world. Since we see the world through ideology—through various and often contradictory narratives, it is possible for people to see the same act and yet perceive very different things.

The O. J. Simpson case serves as an obvious example of this point. Sociologist Darnell M. Hunt argues that blacks and whites produced very different interpretations of the O. J. Simpson trial, suggesting that "race shape[s] the perception of 'reality.'"[9] While a majority of black respondents considered Simpson not guilty, the majority of white respondents pronounced him guilty. Hunt asserts that a history of different social realities experienced by black and white Americans produces "raced ways of seeing"[10] and accounts for the divergent interpretations of the trial.

In my research I employ a deconstructionist approach, which has particular consequences for the discipline. Sociology has thought itself distinct from the humanities because it sets out to study social reality, rather than to explore what are considered simply texts: *representations* of reality. Ann Game points out, however, that deconstruction breaches these disciplinary boundaries, arguing that reality itself is written within cultural systems. "In this view the social world does not consist of ready-made objects that are put into representation."[11] It is important to note, however, that deconstructing the text/reality dichotomy does not mean abandoning any attempt to understand reality. Instead, it means revealing the opposition between the two as a human construction and breaking down that opposition: reality itself is textual, and texts are real.

In *Reading Rodney King/Reading Urban Uprising*, Kimberlè Crenshaw and Gary Peller assert that to explore race in America, it is imperative to "examine critically how ideological narratives work as a form of social power."[12] Extending this approach to the study of race, they suggest that "the realm of interpretation, ideology, and narrative is a critical site in the production of American racial domination. . . . At stake . . . is a contest over which, and whose, narrative structure will prevail in the interpretation of events in the social world."[13] Rather than seeing ideological narratives as mystifications of the truth, this approach emphasizes that all seeing takes place within a narrative field. Every act of seeing is an ideological reading "in the sense that the narrative lines shape what and how events are perceived in the first place."[14]

The power of ideology comes from its power to define what it does and does not make sense to say, the power to define knowledge and reality. As Stuart Hall argues, this is the power "of representing the order of things which endow[s] its limiting perspectives with that natural or divine inevitability which makes them appear universal, natural and coterminous with 'reality' itself."[15]

Frequently, ideology and discourse are posited as distinct from the oppression and material reality of bodies and subjects. However, analyzing gender oppression, Denise Riley explains,

> The unmet needs and sufferings do not spring from a social reality of oppression, which has to be posed against what is said and written about women—but that they spring from the ways in which women are positioned . . . as "women." This positioning occurs both in language, forms of description, and what gets carried out, so that it is misleading to set up a combat for superiority between the two.[16]

If race and gender are social constructs, racialized, gendered bodies do not exist outside of discourse, they are discursive effects.

The collected essays in *Reading Rodney King/Reading Urban Uprising* demonstrate this point. They emphasize the textual nature of reality, contesting the dominant representation of the Rodney King incident and providing counterreadings. The jury's verdict in the trial of the police officers who beat King came as a shock to many. The reality of the beating seemed so clear, so obvious; how could the jury have possibly believed that it was King, and not the police, who was the source of danger? How could they believe, as one juror surmised, that King was "in 'total control' of the situation?"[17] As Judith Butler asserts, what the trial and its horrific conclusions teach us is that there is no simple recourse to the visible, to visual evidence, that it still and always calls to be read, that it is already a reading. . . . It is not, then, a question of negotiating between what is "seen," on the one hand, and a "reading" which is imposed upon the visual evidence, on the other. . . . The visual field is not neutral to the question of race; it is itself a racial formation.[18]

Seeing, then, is always also a reading. We do not have unmediated access to an independently existing reality. Instead, what is seen and what gets seen are themselves textual productions, with very real consequences, as the Rodney King trial certainly reminds us.

With its long tradition of politically motivated research, sociology is particularly amenable to poststructuralist theory.[19] Embedded within the sociological tradition is a concern with social change: sociology not just for its own sake, but for improving people's lives. This is certainly what drew me to sociology in the first place. The rise of a specifically feminist sociology has furthered this endeavor, interrogating the whole notion of an objective sociology and our subject/object dichotomy, which assumes that the researcher exists in a relation of externality to the object of study.[20] A poststructuralist approach has the potential to further this project and to further politicize sociology and the relationship between sociologist and subject. By highlighting the knowledge/power connection, poststructuralism draws attention to the role of the sociologist in *producing* reality.[21]

From this starting point, I see the white supremacist movement itself as a discursive construct. Scholars, journalists, and tracking organizations, as well as movement participants themselves, all take part in producing the reality of the white supremacist movement. In approaching reality as a series of texts to be read, we become aware of our own role in constructing that reality. There are various ways to demarcate and read white supremacist discourse, and each will produce different kinds of knowledge, with different political implications.

The way in which we approach and define the white supremacist movement has consequences for how we view race and racism more generally. Contemporary analyses continue to focus on what makes the movement extremist and to explore the key players and events.[22] As Suzanne Harper notes, traditional studies of white supremacist movement have attempted to explain who joins these organizations and why.[23] Treating these organizations as "extremist" groups, research often focuses on questions such as these: Who joins these movements and what characteristics distinguish them?[24] How can we define an extremist movement and extremist ideology?[25] What characteristics of a society encourage or discourage the development and growth of such movements?[26] What has been the historical development of this movement?[27] What factors do the various white supremacist groups have in common?[28] What danger does the movement present to society?[29] Tracking organizations, like the Anti-Defamation League, the Center for Democratic Renewal, the Northwest Coalition against Malicious Harassment, Political Research Associates, and the Southern Poverty Law Center, follow and document the organization, leadership, and activities of white supremacist organizations, recording their violent histories.

The tendency to focus on leaders in a particular movement, and to explore the character traits that lead individuals to join this movement, contributes to the belief that racism is something rooted in one's personality, rather than institutionalized in our society and culture at every level, shaping the lives of everyone. Defining white supremacy as extremist in its racism often has the result of absolving the mainstream population of its racism, portraying white supremacists as the racist fringe in contrast to some nonracist majority.[30] As David Theo Goldberg suggests,

> racist expressions are generally reduced to personal prejudices of individuals, to irrational appeals. . . . Racism is considered a premodern prejudice, one that enlightened modern meliorism takes itself to be overcoming through the force of reason. . . . One finds this paradigm reflected in the contemporary popular and academic reduction of racial concerns to the irrational prejudices of "hate crimes" and "hate offenses."[31]

I have chosen, instead, not to approach my research as a study of an extremist hate movement, in all of its uniqueness, but to approach contemporary white supremacist discourse as an example of racist discourse. This is not to suggest that white supremacist discourse is the same as, or representative of, all racial discourse, nor to suggest that research that emphasizes the differences between the two are not important, but instead to open up new areas for discussion. The relationship between the white supremacist movement and the mainstream is one that needs to be rethought. Particularly in light of the increasing violence of the movement, this project has crucial and immediate importance.

The mainstream/white supremacist opposition has been used strategically for political purposes. Defining the white supremacist movement as a "lunatic fringe"[32] enables us to demonize them and define their project as illegitimate. For example, John George and Laird Wilcox title their book *Nazis, Communists, Klansmen, and Others on the Fringe*.[33] This approach can be useful, so I do not want to suggest that this style of reading is inappropriate. However, traditional research has not suggested that the study of the white supremacist movement can increase our knowledge or understanding of the mainstream, and it is only recently that some scholars have begun to point out the connections between them.[34] Zygmunt Bauman has observed a similar approach in traditional studies of the Holocaust. As he observes,

> Traditional sociological studies of the Holocaust approach it as a "one item set," a one-off episode, which perhaps sheds some light on the *pathology* of the society in which it occurred, but hardly adds anything to our understanding of this society's *normal* state.[35]

He suggests, however, that the Holocaust is

> more than a deviation from an otherwise straight path of progress . . . in short, the Holocaust was not an antithesis of modern civilization and everything (or so we like to think) it stands for. We suspect (even if we refuse to admit it) that the Holocaust could merely have uncovered another face of the same modern society whose other, more familiar, face we so admire. And that the two faces are perfectly comfortably attached to the same body.[36]

Bauman's observations seem particularly relevant to the study of the contemporary white supremacist movement. Rather than representing the "antithesis of modern civilization," as it is so often depicted in the media, the contemporary white supremacist movement is based on the very same tenets of modern, Enlightenment discourse that ground mainstream assumptions about race and gender.[37] As Cornel West asserts,

> the very structure of modern discourse *at its inception* produced forms of rationality, scientificity, and objectivity as well as aesthetic and cultural ideals which require the constitution of the idea of white supremacy. This requirement follows from a logic endemic to the very structure of modern discourse.[38]

Western Enlightenment thought has concerned itself with defining and knowing the other as a method of social control. As Susan Hekman elaborates,

> The discussion of women from the Greeks onward has focused on the effort to define the essential nature of woman and thereby to determine her proper social role. This effort is an outgrowth of the foundational, essentialist impulse that has characterized western philosophy since its inception.[39]

White supremacist as well as mainstream discourse assumes that race and gender differences are rooted in nature. While there are certainly widely differing beliefs about the significance and meaning of difference, the assumption that difference is ontologically given is taken for granted.

The construction of racial differences is central to racism.[40] The study of the white supremacist movement, then, is not only the study of racist ideology, but of the construction of races themselves. This highlights another important difference in my approach: rather than reading this discourse as one that is *descriptive* of race, I am reading it as one that actively *constructs* race. Representations of the white supremacist movement traditionally define it as one that attempts to champion white interests while espousing hatred toward blacks and Jews, taking the given reality of race for granted. Instead, I read this movement as actively producing the differences that it seeks to exploit. Deconstructing our taken for granted text/reality distinction shows the reality of race to be one that is constantly being written and read.

If we accept that race is socially constructed, then we must recognize our own research and writing as one site of that construction. Studies of the white supremacist movement that uncritically take race as a given reality contribute to the reification of race as a foundation beyond critical interrogation.[41] This approach contributes to the white supremacist project itself: the project of constructing racial difference and hierarchy as a given reality.

While the work of Kathleen Blee[42] is one of the few attempts to document the role and activities of women in the American white supremacist movement, most research on white supremacy has failed to address issues of gender. The recent work of Jessie Daniels further contributes to a feminist analysis of the movement, exploring the intersections of race and gender in depictions of white men and women, black men and women, and Jewish men and women in contemporary white supremacist discourse.[43] I hope to take the analysis of gender further, going beyond simply describing gendered images in white supremacist ideology and exploring, instead, the intertwined construction of race and gender as well as how race and gender work in this discourse to make certain ways of seeing and understanding the world possible. I argue that white supremacist discourse is about redefining masculinity. Gender is clearly integral to white supremacist ideology, and that is one of my central arguments throughout this book.

White supremacist publications provide the ideal site to explore the construction of race and gender in discourse on interracial sexuality. Interracial sexuality emerges as the central issue in white supremacist discourse, and we shall explore why. While considered extremist in their beliefs, the white supremacists construct identity based on modern Enlightenment conceptions of identity that have been taken for granted by mainstream discourse. White supremacist beliefs are rooted historically in mainstream American beliefs about the significance of race and the necessity of racial segregation. While white supremacists are usually labeled extremist for their support of violence, most hate crimes are not performed by members of white supremacist groups.

White supremacist antagonism toward interracial sexuality is also not as extreme as we might expect, especially when viewed within the context of American history. Prior to the 1967 U.S. Supreme Court ruling in *Loving v. Virginia*, seventeen states had laws against interracial marriage. At one point, forty of the fifty states banned interracial marriage.[44] Interracial sexuality remains controversial. Today, interracial marriages constitute only about 2 percent of all marriages,[45] suggesting that strong cultural taboos against intermarriage still exist. The vast majority of these marriages, however, occur between white and nonblack others. In fact, marriages between whites and nonblack others are three times more likely than marriages between whites and blacks, and respondents to a Knight-Ridder poll were most approving of marriages between "other combinations of races, and were least critical of Asian and Hispanic unions."[46] Clearly, black/white relations remain the most problematic.

Each year, dozens of television talk shows focus on the "problems" of interracial dating, interracial marriage, mixed-race adoptions, etc. Numerous movies have focused on this "problem," ranging from *Imitation of Life* and *Guess Who's Coming To Dinner* to the more recent *Jungle Fever, Mississippi Masala, Made in America*, and *Secrets and Lies*. These texts both illustrate and recreate the Western preoccupation with interracial sexuality, and my analysis will explore just why interracial sexuality plays such an integral role in white supremacist discourse and, especially, in the construction of racialized, gendered identities. Interracial sexuality is not simply one among many issues that preoccupy white supremacists; it is my contention that the issue of interracial sexuality is key to comprehending the white supremacist worldview. As Patricia J. Williams argues, it is essential that we explore the "metaphors [that] mask the hierarchies that make racial domination frequently seems so 'natural,' so invisible, indeed so attractive."[47] Interracial sexuality is one of those metaphors.

Chapter two will expand the contours of my theoretical approach, critiquing the traditional social science literature on interracial relationships and providing an overview of contemporary theoretical perspectives that advance the notion that race and gender are interconnected social constructs. I will also introduce the relevant work of cultural critics whose theories I draw upon to explore the production of racialized, gendered identities in white supremacist discourse. Chapter three locates white supremacist conceptions of race squarely within mainstream American racial history, exploring the development of the concept of race and highlighting the centrality of the regulation of interracial sexuality to definitions of racial identity and the maintenance of white privilege. In chapter four I provide a brief overview of the history of the U.S. white supremacist movement as well as the development and context of the contemporary movement. This chapter presents a demographic picture of the movement and discusses the range of publications analyzed throughout this book. My analysis of white supremacist publications begins in chapter five, where I explore the construction of race and gender as heritable, permanent essences. Chapters six and seven analyze the widespread obsession with interracial relationships throughout white supremacist discourse and discuss the deployment of interracial imagery as a metaphor for all threats to racial and gender boundaries. Chapter eight further explores the threat of boundary transgressions through images of those who straddle or threaten to disrupt those borders: "mongrels," Jews, and those considered improperly gendered. These figures serve as threats of punishment that reinforce properly racialized and gendered subject positions. Finally, in chapter nine, I explore white supremacist solutions to the problem of border maintenance and their central goal of forging and privileging white masculinity.

I have filled this book with the words and images of white supremacy, incorporating excerpts and illustrations from the publications I review. I hope these powerful examples will make the white supremacist worldview real for readers. I do not think my own words could be adequate to summarize the breadth of anger, fear, confusion, and dedication expressed by the authors of these publications. Many of these excerpts are disturbing and difficult to read. Having immersed myself in the writings of white supremacists for the past five years, I now find it difficult to block these white supremacist voices out of my head. I find that I am always thinking about how white supremacists would think about any given event. As the O. J. Simpson trial preoccupied the nation, I was constantly imagining the headlines and articles that I knew must be filling white supremacist newsletters, warning of the dangers for white women who wed black males. I have learned, in a way, to think like a white supremacist. While I find this extremely disturbing, it is a forceful and constant reminder of just how powerful discourse is in shaping the way we interpret events and of the various interpretations available. White supremacist discourse is highly flexible and nebulous, changing to respond to any issue. Any event, any question, any piece of history, can be manipulated to fit into its broad conspiracy theory. I hope that understanding how this discourse works will foster more successful and strategic responses.

NOTES

1. *Instauration* January 1977, 10–11.
2. *Instauration* August 1976, 5.
3. Frankenberg 1993; Morrison 1992.
4. Morrison 1992, 11.
5. Lucal 1996, 246.
6. Ignatiev and Garvey 1996; Lipsitz 1995; Roediger 1991; Saxton 1987.
7. Frankenberg 1993; Harper 1993; Roediger 1991; Sacks 1994; Saxon 1987.
8. Berger and Luckmann 1966; Garfinkel 1967.
9. Hunt 1996, 2.
10. Hunt 1996.
11. Game 1991, 4.
12. Crenshaw and Peller 1993, 62.
13. Crenshaw and Peller 1993, 57.
14. Crenshaw and Peller 1993, 60.
15. Hall 1982, 65.

16. Riley 1988, 2.
17. Butler 1993b, 15.
18. Butler 1993b, 17.
19. Brewer 1989.
20. Harding 1986; Collins 1990; Smith 1987.
21. Foucault 1978; Game 1991; Seidman 1991; Webster 1992.
22. Ezekiel 1995; George and Wilcox 1992.
23. Harper 1993.
24. Aho 1990; Bell 1964; Blee 1991a, 1995, 1996; Ezekiel 1995; Langer 1990; Lipset and Raab 1970; Maclean 1994; Marks 1996; Sims 1978.
25. Aho 1990; George and Wilcox 1992; Lipset and Raab 1970.
26. Bell 1964; Blee 1995; Jenness and Broad 1997; Lipset and Raab 1970; Moore 1991; Wade 1987.
27. Anti-Defamation League 1988a, 1988b, 1995, 1996a; Bell 1964; Blee 1991b; Chalmers 1987; Diamond 1995; Lipset and Raab 1970; Maclean 1994; Marks 1996; Moore 1991; Omi 1991; Wade 1987.
28. Anti-Defamation League 1988b, 1996a; Aho 1994; Ezekiel 1995; George and Wilcox 1992; Marks 1996.
29. Anti-Defamation League 1988b, 1991, 1995, 1996a; Coates 1987; Dees 1996; Jenness and Broad 1997; Marks 1996; Wade 1987.
30. Ferber 1992.
31. Goldberg 1993, 7.
32. Ridgeway 1990.
33. George and Wilcox 1992.
34. See, for example: Daniels 1997; Ezekiel 1995; Feagin and Vera 1995; Omi 1991.
35. Bauman 1989, 7.
36. Bauman 1989, 7.
37. Goldberg 1993.
38. West 1982, 47.
39. Hekman 1990, 136.
40. Goldberg 1993; West 1989.
41. Goldberg 1993; Webster 1992.
42. Blee 1991a, 1991b, 1995.
43. Daniels 1997.
44. Young 1995, 148.
45. Davis 1991.
46. Arnett and Pugh, 1997.
47. Williams 1997, 15.

2

READING RACE AND GENDER

Sociologists have long been interested in the phenomena of intimate interracial relationships, particularly for what they can tell us about race relations more generally. Michael C. Kearl and Edward Murguia explain that "one widely recognized indicator of minority assimilation into the majority society is the intermarriage between minority and majority groups."[1] From an assimilationist perspective, intermarriage is a significant indicator of the incorporation of minorities into the dominant society.

While I find an assimilationist framework problematic, I too believe that the study of interracial relationships has consequences for our understanding of broader race relations. And while this book focuses on the discussion of interracial sexuality in white supremacist discourse only, there are implications for the ways we make sense of interracial relationships and the fear of interracial sexuality more generally, as well as for our understanding of race.

A great deal of sociological research has focused on the "problem" of interracial relationships. The literature is generally subsumed under the study of intermarriage, which deals with interracial, interethnic, and interreligious unions. A large body of research in this field is concerned with documenting the number of intermarriages of various groups in various locations.[2] Beyond this, the majority of the sociological theories regarding intermarriage focus on discovering those elements of social structure and culture that shape rates and patterns of intermarriage.

The literature on intermarriage is largely empirical and, by definition, presupposes the existence of discrete racial groups. Little attention is given to what actually constitutes a racial or ethnic group, and studies often rely

upon diverse, sometimes conflicting, indicators. A number of studies rely
upon surname as an indicator of race or ethnicity.[3] For example, most research on Mexican American intermarriage relies upon marriage records as
a data source, and uses "Spanish surname" to represent "Mexican American" or "Hispanic" populations, and "non-Spanish surname" to represent
"Anglo American" populations. As authors Murguia and W. Parker Frisbie
admit, " 'Anglo' is often used somewhat loosely in this type of analysis and,
not infrequently, becomes a residual category for all persons not explicitly
identified as having a Spanish surname."[4] Other research relies upon birth-
place. For example, in one study, if the bride, groom, or any of their parents
were born "in Puerto Rico, Cuba, the Dominican Republic, Mexico, or a
Spanish speaking Central or South American country" the individual is labeled Hispanic.[5]

While a great deal of attention is given to defining or measuring a racial
or ethnic community, it is assumed that discrete races exist and how to best
represent and measure those racial communities is merely a methodological
problem for social scientists to figure out.

While the sociological literature usually tries to draw implications from
this body of research regarding the relative cohesiveness and solidarity, or
assimilation and breakdown, of racial and ethnic communities, little if any
attention is devoted to considering what constitutes a racial community in
the first place. If race is socially and culturally constructed, and given meaning through discourse, then we, as researchers, contribute to that construction. By failing to explore our own role in the construction of race and
continuing to use it as a category of analysis, we reproduce race as a given,
obvious, natural category, existing outside of discourse, delegitimizing our
very own claims that race is socially constructed.

The Racialization of America, by Yehudi O. Webster, provides an important critique of the role of the social sciences in the processes of racialization
and the failure of social scientists to recognize and examine this role. As
Webster asserts,

> it is neither race nor racism that bedevils American society, but rather
> that racial classification enjoys a privileged status in social studies. . . .
> References to its realness are meant to consolidate and perpetuate its
> presence as something that cannot, or should not, be questioned.[6]

In failing to examine their role in the construction of race, sociological studies that examine race relations reproduce the assumption of a biological

basis for race. Webster suggests that "much of the controversy over the significance of racism can be avoided by conceiving racial classification *itself* as racism."[7] Webster's book is important in that it directs us to turn our attention to the social construction of race, highlighting the centrality of racial classification to racism. The relationship between racial classification and racism is one that is seldom explored, yet racism requires the concept of race, and the history of the two are intertwined.

AN ALTERNATIVE THEORETICAL PERSPECTIVE: THE SOCIAL CONSTRUCTION OF RACE AND GENDER

In contrast to widely assumed essentialist notions, the most exciting recent research on race refuses to take racial categorizations for granted, exploring instead their social construction.[8] Ken Clatterbaugh defines essentialism as the assumption that "social differences such as those between men and women, people of different races, or social classes are due to intrinsic biological or psychic differences between the members of the different groups."[9] These differences are believed to be innate and unchanging and are seen as more significant than environmental factors in explaining differences among people.

Essentialism, however, cannot be supported. While our commonsense assumptions may tell us that race is rooted in biology, biologists today reject such notions.[10] Racial categories lack any scientific foundation; there is greater genetic variety within racial groups than between them, and racial classifications vary both cross-culturally and historically.[11] While these arguments go back at least as far as W. E. B. DuBois, they have found full elaboration in recent theory. Michael Omi and Howard Winant argue convincingly that race is a "pre-eminently sociohistorical concept. Racial categories and the meaning of race," they explain, "are given concrete expression by the specific social relations and historical context in which they are embedded."[12] Following this lead, a body of research that explores the construction of racialized identities in various historical contexts is accumulating.[13]

While it is popular today in academia to study racial "diversity," this approach often ends up reifying racial categorizations.[14] Alternatively, a social constructionist approach emphasizes the critical need for researchers to "read the processes of differentiation, not look for differences."[15] As Omi and Winant suggest, the meaning of race and racialized meanings are politically contested, and it is this contested terrain that needs to be explored. Processes of racialization are always political because the elaboration of race takes place within relations of power and privilege. The project of exploring the historical, social construction of race is at the same time an exploration of racist culture and practice.[16]

Because race is a construction, it is often intertwined with the construction of other identity categories, especially gender. Linda Nicholson suggests that feminism has at times embraced two different notions of gender. The first usage of gender refers to behaviors and personality traits, often conceptualized as the product of socialization processes, which are juxtaposed with the notion of a biologically sexed body. According to this usage, Nicholson suggests that sexed bodies are analogous to a coatrack, upon which different cultures throw different articles of clothing. While gender is defined as a cross-cultural variable according to this view, the biological coatrack is taken as a given foundation.

Moving away from the biological determinism of this perspective, the second understanding of gender subsumes the notion of sex. Rejecting the notion of sexed bodies that exist outside of the social, this view defines gender as "any social construction having to do with the male/female distinction, including those constructions that separate 'female' bodies from 'male' bodies . . . the body is itself always seen through social interpretation."[17] This perspective does not ignore or negate the body; instead, the body is no longer seen as a stable and given foundation that can ground claims about gender. The body itself becomes a social variable.[18]

Expanding a perspective that posits sexed bodies themselves as social constructs, Joan W. Scott defines gender as the

> social organization of sexual difference. But this does not mean that gender reflects or implements fixed and natural physical differences between women and men; rather gender is the knowledge that establishes meanings for bodily differences.[19]

Scott argues that our knowledge of sexual differences is never "pure," but always shaped by broader cultural systems. In his study *Making Sex: Body and Gender from the Greeks to Freud*, Thomas Laqueur has demonstrated that Western conceptions of human sexual anatomy and sexual difference have changed drastically throughout history. There is no direct access to the body then, outside of cultural contexts.[20]

As Nicholson elaborates, feminist analyses that rely upon the first understanding of gender can be characterized as a "feminism of difference," highlighting the differences between women and men. A "feminism of
difference," however, is at the same time a "feminism of uniformity," posit-
ing some common essence among women that "tend[s] to reflect the perspective of those making the characterizations."[21] Women of color have
charged that this basis for commonality assumes a white, heterosexual,
upper middle-class ideal.[22] This perspective, in fact, ignores differences
among women. If sexed bodies are themselves productions, then if and how
they are produced varies and must be interconnected with the production
of bodily subjects more generally and with other categories of identity that
also take part in producing bodies. Analyzing the social construction of gender, therefore, means taking seriously the intersections of gender, race, and
other constructed categories of identity and difference. Elizabeth Spelman
highlights this when she points out how "crucial gender distinctions can be
to the maintenance of . . . race distinctions . . . [and] the study of gender
relations is absolutely essential to the study of . . . race relations because it
is pivotal to the study of how societies define and distinguish themselves."[23]

RACE, GENDER, AND SUBJECT PRODUCTION

Judith Butler expands our understanding of the construction of gender,
demonstrating that the production of subjects actually occurs through the
construction of gendered identities. She contends that those practices that
regulate the construction of coherent gender identities constitute our very
understandings of identity itself. "It would be wrong," she warns, "to think
that the discussion of 'identity' ought to proceed prior to a discussion of
gender identity for the simple reason that 'persons' only become intelligible
through becoming gendered in conformity with recognizable standards of
gender intelligibility."[24] It is the regulation of compulsory heterosexuality
that produces the illusion of coherent gender identities. The production of
gender occurs through the performance of heterosexuality; motivating this
performance is the threat of punishment, symbolized by "at least two inar-
ticulate figures of abject homosexuality, the feminized fag and the phallic-
ized dyke."[25] Those who do not partake in the heterosexual performance are
seen as not properly gendered. Sexuality becomes the performance of one's
gender.

What it means to be human is constrained and defined by norms of cultural intelligibility. In other words, our cultural norms make certain forms of living and being comprehensible, while at the same time making other forms unimaginable. Those who do not conform to these cultural norms are frequently excluded, attacked, and denied rights. Yet these abjected identities are central to the definition of normal subjectivity. It is against this realm of the abject that the normal is defined, maintained, and privileged. Butler demonstrates one example of an abjected identity in heterosexuality's delegitimization of homosexuality.

Building upon Butler's insights, I explore the production of gendered subjects through the institution of heterosexuality, but I argue that this is also a *racialized* process. In white supremacist discourse, the regulation of sexuality is governed not only by a compulsory heterosexuality, but by a compulsory intraracial sexuality, which desires to maintain the illusion of racial purity and secure racial boundaries.[26]

Butler demonstrates the production of culturally intelligible gender identities, suggesting that unintelligible, abject identities, those not fully human, are simultaneously produced; I read Omi and Winant as suggesting that there is a similar process at work in the production of coherent racial identities. They point out that

> one of the first things we notice about people when we meet them . . .
> is their race. We utilize race to provide clues about *who* a person is.
> This fact is made painfully obvious when we encounter someone
> whom we cannot conveniently racially categorize—someone who is,
> for example, racially "mixed" or of an ethnic/racial group with which
> we are not familiar. Such an encounter becomes a source of discomfort and momentarily a crisis of racial meaning. Without a racial identity, one is in danger of having no identity.[27]

Racialized identities govern our notions of what it means to be human. As this passage suggests, the production of recognizable racial identities, like the production of recognizable gender identities, requires the simultaneous production of "unviable (un)subjects,"[28] in this case, mixed-race individuals.

Butler's theory is informative for my research because it provides a theoretical vehicle for interpreting the construction of white masculinity in white supremacist discourse, as well as the ever attendant threat of interracial sexuality. Within white supremacist discourse, the regulation of heterosexual and intraracial sexuality produces culturally intelligible, racialized, and gendered identities, while at the same time relegating homosexuals, Jews, and mixed-race people to the realm of the unlivable. Butler argues that this type of exclusion is a key point of deconstruction often overlooked by constructionist approaches. While constructionist analyses often argue that everything is discursively constructed, the construction of the human is always in relation to its constitutive outside, a realm of beings *not* constructed as human.[29]

DECONSTRUCTING THE BOUNDARIES: THE REGULATION OF INTERRACIAL SEXUALITY

The deconstruction of binary oppositions directs our attention to borders and boundaries. In any given binary opposition, it is the border between the two terms that constructs them as apparently coherent and stable identities. For example, the historical construction of the opposition white/black involves defining the limits of whiteness and blackness and defining precisely who qualifies as white and who qualifies as black. In order to produce whiteness as a stable, natural, given identity, the boundaries of whiteness must be specified and secured. For example, chapter three will explore the preoccupation with mulattoes, those at the border of the white/black dichotomy, which lies at the center of the construction of scientific racial classifications in the eighteenth and nineteenth centuries. In order to racially classify the population, scientists, politicians, and the courts found it necessary to specifically delineate who was white and who was black. This was done over the years with laws labeling the fraction of black blood necessary to deem an individual black. This act of boundary maintenance was necessary to construct racial categories. Whenever pressure to produce secure racial classifications increased, public outcry over interracial sexuality also increased. Interracial sexuality and the births of mulattoes represented boundary crossings that were widely perceived as threatening otherwise stable racial boundaries.

Deconstruction directs us to interrogate the pivotal position of boundaries in constructing identities. As Iris Marion Young explains, "any move to define an identity, a closed totality, always depends on excluding some elements, separating the pure from the impure . . . the logic of identity seeks to keep those borders firmly drawn."[30] The construction of racial identities, then, requires a policing of the borders, a maintenance of the boundaries between "one's own kind" and others. Regulations prohibiting interracial sexual relationships actually serve to produce and consolidate racial identities. It is through the construction of boundaries themselves that identities come into existence. Butler points out this central insight of deconstruction: " 'Inner' and 'outer' make sense only with reference to a mediating boundary that strives for stability. . . . Hence, 'inner' and 'outer' constitute a binary distinction that stabilizes and consolidates the coherent subject."[31]

When I began exploring white supremacist discourse in the newsletters and publications of its organizations, I found interracial sexuality referred to and discussed over and over again, in places where it did not seem to make sense. I did not understand how the image of interracial sexuality was being used. There were places where references to it seemed ridiculous to me, for example, in discussions of affirmative action or women in the workplace. Arguments that claimed that affirmative action would lead to interracial sexuality and, even further, that the real goal of affirmative action is increasing interracial sexuality seemed preposterous (and still do). But in exploring what interracial sexuality means in this discourse, how it comes to signify the erasure of all difference, and how threats to hierarchy become defined as threats to difference, I began to see why this makes sense to the writers and readers of white supremacist discourse. Certain ways of seeing are made possible, while other ways excluded.

A deconstructive discourse analysis enables me to explore the production of meaning in contemporary white supremacist discourse. Interracial sexuality remains taboo among the public at large but is a particularly disturbing threat to the white supremacist movement. Why? What power relations are threatened by interracial sexuality? Throughout this discourse, interracial sexuality is presented as the enemy of everything white supremacists desire. For white supremacists, the construction of racial purity requires a policing of the racial boundaries; interracial sexuality is the greatest threat to this border maintenance. For a movement concerned with forging a white identity, interracial sexuality is constructed as a threat to the boundaries of whiteness, to the very possibility of a white identity.

NOTES

1. Kearl and Murguia 1985, 453.
2. Cazares, Murguia, and Frisbie 1984; Kitano and Chai 1982; Kitano and Yeung 1982; Monahan 1976b.

3. Cazares, Murguia, and Frisbie 1984; Kearl and Murguia 1985; Kitano and Chai 1982; Kitano and Yeung 1982.
4. Murguia and Frisbie 1977, 375.
5. Gurak and Fitzpatrick 1982, 923.
6. Webster 1992, 2.
7. Webster 1992, 11.
8. Balibar and Wallerstein 1991; Goldberg 1993; Hall 1990; Omi and Winant 1986; Shanklin 1994; Young 1995.
9. Clatterbaugh 1995, 49.
10. Marks 1994, 35.
11. Davis 1995; Moore 1995; Omi and Winant 1986; Young 1995.
12. Omi and Winant 1986, 60.
13. Goldberg 1993; Harper 1993; Morrison 1992; Roediger 1991; Saxton 1987.
14. Carby 1992; Webster 1992.
15. Crosby 1992, 140.
16. Goldberg 1993; Young 1995.
17. Nicholson 1994, 79.
18. Hubbard 1992; Laqueur 1990; Nicholson 1994.
19. Scott 1988b, 2.
20. Laqueur 1990.
21. Nicholson 1994, 94.
22. Collins 1990; Garcia 1990; hooks 1984; Nicholson 1994; Spelman 1988.
23. Spelman 1988, 168–69.
24. Butler 1991, 17.
25. Butler 1993a, 102.
26. Butler 1993a, 18.
27. Omi and Winant 1986, 62.
28. Butler 1991, 20.
29. Butler 1993a, 8.
30. Young 1990, 303.
31. Butler 1990, 134.

3

PLANTING THE SEED

The Invention of Race

If race is constructed differently in different times and places, we must explore its construction within specific historical contexts. While the primary objective of this book is to deconstruct racial identity in contemporary white supremacist discourse, white supremacist definitions of race, and acute fears of interracial relationships, to a large extent reflect and rearticulate historically predominant racial ideologies in the United States. The obsession with race-mixing and mixed-race peoples exhibited in white supremacist discourse has been a recurrent theme throughout the history of Western racial ideology. A brief review of the history of the concept of race, and concomitant beliefs about race-mixing, is important to my argument because it illuminates the mainstream origins of contemporary white supremacist racial ideology, as well as the centrality of gender to the ongoing regulation of interracial sexuality.

THE HISTORY OF SCIENTIFIC RACISM

My students are always surprised to learn that race is a relatively recent invention. In their minds, race and racial antagonisms have taken on a universal character; they have always existed, and probably always will, in some form or another. Yet this fatalism belies the reality—that race is indeed a modern concept and, as such, does not have to be a life sentence.

Winthrop Jordan has suggested that ideas of racial inferiority, specifically that blacks were savage and primitive, played an essential role in rationalizing slavery.[1] There was no conception of race as a physical category until the eighteenth century.[2] There was, however, a strong association between blackness and evil, sin, and death, long grounded in European thought. The term "race" is believed to have originated in the Middle Ages in the romance languages, first used to refer to the breeding of animals. Race did not appear in the English language until the sixteenth century and was used as a technical term to define human groups in the seventeenth century. By the end of the eighteenth century, as emphasis upon the observation and classification of human differences grew, "race" became the most commonly employed concept for differentiating human groups according to Northern European standards. Audrey Smedley argues that because "race" has its roots in the breeding of animal stock, unlike other terms used to categorize humans, it came to imply an innate or inbred quality, believed to be permanent and unchanging.[3]

Until the nineteenth century, the Bible was consulted and depended upon for explanations of human variation, and two schools of thought emerged. The first asserted that there was a single creation of humanity, monogenesis, while the second asserted that various human groups were created separately, polygenesis. Polygenesis and ideas about racial inferiority, however, gained few believers, even in the late 1700s when the slave trade was under attack, because few were willing to support doctrines that conflicted with the Bible.[4]

While European Americans remained dedicated to a biblical view of race, the rise of scientific racism in the middle of the eighteenth century shaped debate about the nature and origins of races.[5] The Enlightenment emphasized the scientific practices of observing, collecting evidence, measuring bodies, and developing classificatory schemata. In the early stages of science, the most prevalent activity was the collection, examination, and arrangement of data into categories. Carolus Linnaeus, a prominent naturalist in the eighteenth century, developed the first authoritative racial division of humans in his *Natural System*, published in 1735.[6] Considered the founder of scientific taxonomy, he attempted to classify all living things, plant and animal, positioning humans within the matrix of the natural world. As Cornel West demonstrates, from the very beginning, racial classification has always involved hierarchy and the linkage of physical features with character and cultural traits.[7] For example, in the descriptions of his racial classifications, Linnaeus defines Europeans as "gentle, acute, inventive . . .

governed by customs," while Africans are "crafty, indolent, negligent . . . governed by caprice."[8] Like most scientists of his time, however, Linnaeus considered all humans part of the same species, the product of a single creation.

Linnaeus was followed by Georges Louis Leclerc, Comte de Buffon, who is credited with introducing the term "race" into the scientific lexicon. Buffon also believed in monogenesis and in his 1749 publication *Natural History*, suggested that human variations were the result of differences in environment and climate. Whiteness, of course, was assumed to be the real color of humanity. Buffon suggested that blacks became dark-skinned because of the hot tropical sun and that if they moved to Europe, their skin would eventually lighten over time. Buffon cited interfertility as proof that human races were not separate species, establishing this as the criterion for distinguishing a species.

Buffon and Johann Friedrich Blumenbach are considered early founders of modern anthropology. Blumenbach advanced his own systematic racial classification in his 1775 study *On the Natural Varieties of Mankind*, designating five human races: Caucasian, Mongolian, Ethiopian, American, and Malay. While he still considered races to be the product of one creation, he ranked them on a scale according to their distance from the "civilized" Europeans.[9] He introduced the term "Caucasian," chosen because he believed that the Caucasus region in Russia produced the world's most beautiful women. This assertion typifies the widespread reliance upon aesthetic judgments in ranking races. West asserts that the tremendous influence of the classical revival upon Enlightenment thought embedded classical ideals of beauty and proportion within science. Ancient Greeks were believed to represent the ideal, and they became the standard against which other peoples were literally measured. West argues that the role of Greek classical aesthetics and cultural norms in shaping modern scientific discourse about race cannot be underestimated. In the work of Blumenbach,

> the aesthetic criteria and cultural ideals of ancient Greece began to come to the forefront . . . he praised the symmetrical face as the most beautiful . . . precisely because it approximated . . . the proper anatomical proportions found in Greek sculpture.[10]

The science of racial classifications relied upon ideals of Greek beauty, as well as culture, as a standard by which to measure races. Race became central to the definition of Western culture, which became synonomous with "civilization."[11]

Scientific theories of race failed to gain widespread acceptance and importance until 1865, with the emancipation and rise of blacks as a strong political force.[12] At this point, the scientific concept of race was at its peak. Humans were understood generally as a single species consisting of a set number of races with varying abilities and dispositions. It was believed that "human affairs could be understood only if individuals were seen as representatives of races, for it was there that the driving forces of human history resided."[13]

While the theory of monogenesis maintained its stronghold, many prominent American scientists began to argue forcefully for the theory of polygenesis in the early to mid-nineteenth century. Most prominent among these were Louis Agassiz and Samuel George Morton. Agassiz developed a theory of separate centers of creation, suggesting that different species were created separately, in different geographical locations, and argued that migration did not occur to any great extent. He maintained that polygenesis was consistent with the Bible, because the Bible only described the origins of the Caucasians and did not discuss areas of the world unknown to the ancients.[14] Stephen Jay Gould suggests that Agassiz's sexual fears of blacks drove his beliefs. In 1863, Agassiz wrote: "The production of halfbreeds is as much a sin against nature as incest . . . the idea of amalgamation is most repugnant to my feelings, I hold it to be a perversion of every natural sentiment."[15] Conceptions of race were carved out of the fear of interracial sexuality, and ideas about miscegenation from this time are practically indistinguishable from the beliefs of contemporary white supremacists. Agassiz argued for rigid segregation and warned against the dangers of miscegenation:

> Conceive for a moment the difference it would make in future ages, for the prospect of republican institutions and our civilization generally, if instead of the manly population descended from cognate nations the United States should hereafter be inhabited by the effeminate progeny of mixed races. . . . I shudder from the consequences. . . . How shall we eradicate the stigma of a lower race when its blood has once been allowed to flow freely into that of our children.[16]

Whiteness here is tied to masculinity. Gender is often employed as an analogy for racial hierarchy where masculinity symbolizes white superiority, and the downfall of the race is described as a process of feminization.

Morton collected the data to support Agassiz's theory. He amassed hundreds of skulls and devoted himself to determining cranial capacities by measuring the amount of mustard seed or lead shot he could fill the skulls with. In *The Mismeasure of Man*, Gould demonstrates in detail that "Morton's summaries are a patchwork of fudging and finagling in the clear interest of controlling a priori convictions."[17] Morton's publications, however, were the most significant contribution of American polygeny to the project of racial ranking. Morton's conclusions placed Caucasians firmly on top, Indians in the middle, and blacks on the bottom. The influence of his work was widespread, and his studies were reprinted and widely cited as scientific evidence of the unequal mental capacities of the races. Like others who held that races were actually different species, Morton was confronted with the issue of interbreeding. He argued that interfertility be abandoned as a criteria for defining species, claiming that hybridization among different animal species was common in nature.

The issue of miscegenation, and the question of mulattoes, continued to play a central role in scientific theories of race. Any discussion of the existence of races had to address the question of the mixing of races, and any attempt to define the distinctive characteristics of races had also to address the characteristics of the mulatto, the product of racial mixture. Robert J. C. Young argues that "from the 1840s . . . discussions of the question of hybridity became a standard discursive feature of any book on natural history or race, and one of the most persuasive means through which any writer on racial theory established himself as being, in Foucault's phrase, 'in the true.' "[18]

Count Joseph Arthur de Gobineau, in his 1854 *Essay on the Inequality of Human Races*, asserted that race-mixing would inevitably lead to the "deterioration of humanity."[19] It was generally believed that mulattoes were more intelligent than blacks but constitutionally weaker and more susceptible to disease. It was further assumed that, like hybrid species, mulattoes were infertile and therefore inferior to whites and blacks.[20] Nathaniel Southgate Shaler, a leading geologist and paleontologist in the second half of the nineteenth century, believed that blacks, away from the civilizing influence of whites, would revert to barbarism and savagery, conditions he believed to be their heritage and carried in their blood. Because it was assumed that cultural traits were transmitted through blood, Shaler asserted that the superior characteristics of whites would be weakened and overwhelmed by the savage traits of the Negro in any cases of intermixture.[21] Zoologist and paleontologist Edward D. Cope, editor of the *American Naturalist,* wrote in 1890 that "the greatest danger which flows from the presence of the Negro in this country, is the certainty of the contamination of the race."[22] Race was assumed to be an inherited essence, shaping biological, physical, and cultural characteristics.

Debates over monogeny and polygeny were not resolved until the publication of Charles Darwin's theory of evolution. Darwin asserted that races were all evolved from the same organisms and thus were one species. Nevertheless, polygenists shifted the emphasis from creation to evolution, claiming that while there may not have been separate origins, the races had evolved separately. As with many of the arguments discussed here, I found this same argument advanced by contemporary white supremacist publications.

John G. Mencke observes that by the late nineteenth century, three distinct strains of scientific thought molded beliefs about race and race-mixing: Darwinism, Lamarckism, and polygenesis. The surviving ideas of polygenists asserted that each race had an "essence" distinguishing it from other races and accounting for its inferiority or superiority. Lamarckism, an evolutionary environmentalism developed by French naturalist Jean-Baptiste Pierre Antoine Lamarck, suggested that an organism developed the physical means of dealing with its environment and that this ability was then inherited by the offspring.[23] This environmentalism attempted to account for differences in cultural practices, and we find "the interaction of social and biological concepts, as essentially social practices were absorbed and then transmitted by the biological mechanism of Lamarckian heredity."[24] Darwinism provided the final and most important piece, focusing on evolutionary change and highlighting the importance of *controlling* which characteristics should be passed on to future generations and which should be eliminated.[25]

These three perspectives molded both scientific and popular conceptions of race from Reconstruction until World War I, giving rise to social Darwinism and eugenics. Social Darwinists argued, conveniently, that natural selection was at work in the social world and that success was dependent upon one's "fitness." These beliefs supported laissez-faire policies. Herbert Spencer coined the phrase "survival of the fittest" and argued against intervention to help the poor, so that the laws of natural selection could proceed unhindered. The rise of the eugenics movement took this philosophy further, arguing that natural selection should be sped along by policies to encourage the "fit" Northern Europeans and upper classes to reproduce and the sterilization of those defined as "unfit."[26] American and British eugenic theory laid the foundation for Nazi Germany's sterilization and extermination policies in the name of racial purification.

The power of scientific racism lies in the extent to which it shaped popular views on race. The entire Jim Crow system of discrimination and strict segregation was supported by widespread, commonly held scientific assumptions about the permanence of racial essences, the extent to which race determines social and cultural behavior, and the danger of miscegenation.

> Perhaps the most dangerous social implication of scientifically proposed racial classification derives from the power of their supposed genetic basis. . . . Since an individual cannot alter his or her complement of genes, each person is assigned to one category for all eternity.[27]

The history of racial categorizations is intertwined with the history of racism. Science sought to justify a priori racist assumptions and consequently rationalized and greatly expanded the arsenal of racist ideology. Since the eighteenth century, racist beliefs have been built upon scientific racial categorizations and the linking of social and cultural traits to supposed genetic racial differences. While some social critics have suggested that contemporary racism has replaced biology with a concept of culture, the recent publication of *The Bell Curve*[28] attests to the staying power of these genetic notions of race. Today, as in the past, racism weaves together notions of biology and culture, and culture is assumed to be determined by some racial essence.

Science defined race as a concept believed to be hereditary and unalterable. The authority of science contributed to the quick and widespread acceptance of these ideas and prevented their interrogation. Equally important, the study of race and the production of racist theory also helped establish scientific authority and aided discipline builiding. While the history of the scientific concept of race argues that race is an inherent essence, it reveals, on the contrary, that race is a social construct. Young points out that "the different Victorian scientific accounts of race each in their turn quickly became deeply problematic; but what was much more consistent, more powerful and long-lived, was the cultural construction of race."[29]

Because race is not grounded in genetics or nature, the project of defining races always involves drawing and maintaining boundaries between those races. This was no easy task. It is important to pay attention to the construction of those borders: how was it decided, in actual policy, who was considered white and who was considered black? What about those who did not easily fit into either of those categories? What were the dangers of mixing? How could these dangers be avoided? These issues preoccupied policy makers, popular culture, and the public at large.

NEGOTIATING THE BORDERS

From the moment the concept of race was invented, interracial sexuality became a concern. Young observes that "the idea of race here shows itself to be profoundly dialectical: it only works when defined against potential intermixture."[30] Historically, the preoccupation with defining who is white and who is black superceded concern with defining other nonwhites. The history of slavery and Jim Crow segregation depended upon firm knowledge of who was white and black for their support. While at various points in time, concern over defining other nonwhites grew, anxiety over definitions of whiteness and blackness never receded. Defining racial categories is tied to politics and power; for example, the rules defining blacks have always been more stringent than the categorizations of other nonwhites. Historically, it has been easier for those who were the product of white/nonwhite and nonblack intermixture to assimilate, or pass as white, than for those with any black ancestry.

Historian F. James Davis traces this history in his book *Who Is Black? One Nation's Definition*. Davis argues that race-mixing between whites and blacks in the United States became widespread for the first time in Maryland and Virginia in the seventeenth century, occurring largely among white indentured servants and both free and slave blacks. As race-mixing increased, punishments for interracial sexuality were instituted. Interracial sexuality at that time was punishable by whipping and public humiliation. In 1662, Virginia passed the first laws discouraging miscegenation, defining mulattoes born to slave mothers as slaves, and leveling fines on English Christians engaging in interracial sexual relations with black men or women.[31] This represented a significant departure from the tradition of English law, which, until this point, determined lineage through the father. As historian Paula Giddings explains,

The circle of denigration was virtually complete with this law, which managed to combine racism, sexism, greed, and piety. . . . Such legislation laid women open to the most vicious exploitation. For a master could save the cost of buying new slaves by impregnating his own slave, or for that matter having anyone impregnate her. Being able to reproduce one's own labor force would be well worth the fine, even in the unlikely event that it would be imposed.[32]

While these laws encouraged interracial relationships between white male slaveowners and their black female slaves, policy makers sought to discourage interracial liasons between white women and black men. To discourage white women who continued to cohabit with black men, laws were passed in 1681 forcing white women giving birth to mulatto children into five years of servitude, and forcing mulatto children into indentured servitude until age thirty. Additionally, white women engaging in miscegenation faced banishment from the colony.[33]

Increasingly, states moved even further toward the one-drop rule, which defined as black all those with one discernible drop of black blood. With a few exceptions, including Louisiana, which provided mulattoes with an in-between status, the upper South accepted the one-drop rule by the early 1700s.[34] The one-drop rule gained increased acceptance in the lower South as well, because the growth in plantation slavery in the early 1700s prevented widespread race-mixing and most mixing that did occur was between white men and black female slaves. Much of this mixing was through coercion and rape. Angela Davis suggests that sexual coercion was

> an essential dimension of the social relations between slavemaster and slave. In other words, the right claimed by slaveowners and their agents over the bodies of female slaves was a direct expression of their presumed property rights over Black people as a whole.[35]

Interracial sexual relations between white women and black men, however, were not tolerated. The birth of a mulatto child to a slave presented no threat to white dominance and was even an economic asset—an additional slave. A mulatto child born to a white woman, however, was a threat to the entire system of slavery and white supremacy. Because it was assumed that the child of a white woman would remain with its mother, racial segregation would be breached. Gender is central to understanding this distinction. The birth of a mulatto child to a white woman directly usurped white male power and control over both white women and black men. Mulatto children born to black women, on the other hand, were signs of white male power over and rights of access to all women.[36]

As the number of free blacks grew after the American Revolution, whites grew more concerned with ensuring racial boundaries and preventing mulattoes from passing as white. In response to these fears, states throughout the South attempted to define and clearly demarcate who was black and who was white. In 1785, Virginia defined a Negro as someone with at least a single black ancestor in the previous two generations. This rule was adopted by a number of other states. Other states throughout the South and North adopted a stricter version, pushing the boundary to three generations.[37] Throughout the antebellum period, however, skin color played a key role. Lighter-skinned mulattoes were more likely to be free and achieve a higher level of socioeconomic status.[38]

The Civil War and Reconstruction marked a shift in attitudes. By the 1850s, mulattoes lost whatever preferred status they had enjoyed and increasingly sought to ally themselves with the black population. Historians have argued that the declining status of mulattoes was due, to a considerable extent, to rising white fears.[39] For example, Henry Hughes of Mississippi, in an 1854 statement, argued that "Hybridism is heinous. . . . Impurity of races is against the law of nature. Mulattoes are monsters."[40]

With the end of the Civil War in 1865 and the passage of the Thirteenth Amendment, white anxieties rose, and the white population increasingly demanded sharper racial definitions and boundaries. Fears of miscegenation rose among whites, especially in the South, where it was believed that because of the postwar shortage of white males interracial sexual relations between free black males and white females would grow rampant. This fear became an obsession with the burgeoning Ku Klux Klan.[41] Historian Joel Williamson argues that interracial sexual relations actually decreased during the war and Reconstruction as increasing segregation provided fewer opportunities for contact between white women and black men.[42] Nevertheless, fears of miscegenation continued to rise as a response to changing racial relations and black emancipation. Whites continued to join the Klan, and Jim Crow laws were passed with increasing frequency to segregate blacks from whites, limit black political involvement, and prevent blacks from competing economically with whites for jobs.

In his study of the literature of the period, John Mencke highlights the relationship between political, legal, and economic freedom for blacks and its rearticulation as a threat to white womanhood and white racial purity. This connection is made clear in a novel written by Thomas Dixon, published in 1902. In *The Leopard's Spots: A Romance of the White Man's Burden—1865–1900*, Dixon writes,

> The beginning of Negro equality as a vital fact is the beginning of the end of this nation's life. . . . You cannot seek the Negro vote without asking him to your home sooner or later. . . . And if you seat him at your table, he has the right to ask your daughter's hand in marriage.[43]

This fear exemplifies the frequent charge that any freedom for blacks would necessarily and inevitably lead directly to interracial sexual relations between black men and white women.

Throughout the second half of the nineteenth century, discussion of race and racial purity grew increasingly popular in both academic and mainstream circles as Americans developed distinctive beliefs and theories about race for the first time. As scientific beliefs about race were increasingly accepted by the general public, support for the one-drop rule became increasingly universal. Popular opinion grew to support the belief that no matter how white one appeared, if one had a single drop of black blood, no matter how distant, one was black.[44]

After the end of the military occupation of the South, segregation efforts quickened, and between 1880 and 1910 numerous segregation statutes were passed by Southern legislatures. Along with laws requiring separate seating on public transportation and separate public facilities, laws prohibiting interracial marriage were passed. Throughout this period, segregation was enforced through law and the threat and use of violence. Lynching was widespread in the early Jim Crow years but was less necessary in the later years as the Jim Crow system became entrenched. Between 1882 and 1946, close to five thousand people were lynched, an overwhelming number of which were black males. Lynching was most frequently reported as a response to the sexual threat of black males. For example, Emmett Till was lynched in 1955 for reportedly whistling at a white woman.[45] Rape, attempted or actual, of a white woman was the most common offense cited, although these claims usually had no basis in reality. Lynching was often an effort to rescue the reputation of white women who chose to associate with black men, as well as a form of terror aimed at the political and economic advances of blacks.[46]

Angela Davis has argued that the myth of the black male rapist originated at this time as a tool of racist terrorism. As Frederick Douglass pointed out, throughout slavery and the Civil War, this myth was unheard of. "Throughout the entire Civil War, in fact, not a single Black man was publicly accused of raping a white woman."[47] As lynchings became increasingly relied upon as a weapon of political terror, the myth of the black male rapist was embraced as a justification.

> The institution of lynching, in turn, complemented by the continued rape of Black women, became an essential ingredient of the postwar strategy of racist terror. In this way the brutal exploitation of Black labor was guaranteed, and after the betrayal of Reconstruction, the political domination of the Black people as a whole was assured.[48]

The power of this myth was potent, stifling both opposition to individual lynchings and white support for black equality. Anyone who condemned lynching was attacked for failing to protect white womanhood.[49]

The pioneering works of Ida B. Wells, Mary Church Terrell, Frances Harper, Anna Julia Cooper, and other black women at the time drew connections between lynching and rape and the weapons of racism and sexism. As Hazel Carby explains,

> Wells knew that emancipation meant that white men lost their vested interests in the body of the Negro and that lynching and the rape of black women were attempts to regain control. The terrorizing of black communities was a political weapon that manipulated ideologies of sexuality.[50]

Myths of the oversexed black male and female served to justify the lynching of black men and the rape of black women by white men. Wells asserted that while blacks had been granted the right to vote, they were unable to protect that right against such forms of terrorism. She maintained that

> the loss of the vote was both a political silencing and an emasculation which placed black men outside the boundaries of contemporary patriarchal power. . . . Black women were relegated to a place outside the construction of "womanhood." That term included only white women; therefore the rape of black women was of no consequence outside the black community.[51]

As Wells's and Carby's incisive analyses reveal, lynching and rape both served as economic and political weapons against the black community and at the same time defined black men and women as outside of the ideological construction of manhood and womanhood. Carby's analysis also highlights the subordination of white women central to this ideology: "white men used their ownership of the body of the white female as a terrain on which to lynch the black male."[52] The mechanisms of lynching and rape bolstered both racial and gender hierarchies maintaining white male dominance.

As antimiscegenation sentiment reached its peak, concern heightened over recognizing who was black and preventing blacks from passing as whites. Antimiscegenation leagues popped up throughout the South, and beliefs about the inferiority of mulattoes were widespread. This hysteria, however, focused exclusively on preventing and punishing sexual transgressions between black males and white females, and, as during slavery, the

> same male protectors of white womanhood helped mold the Jim Crow practice of sexual exploitation of black females by white males, thus contributing to miscegenation while they were fighting to keep the races pure. This ideological tour de force was accomplished by defining mixed children born to black women as black, as had been done on the slave plantations, thus reinforcing the one-drop rule.[53]

While the one-drop rule became firmly entrenched, white anxiety over "passing" increased. Many Southern whites feared light-skinned mulattoes passing as white and became increasingly paranoid about their own racial identity. Recognizing the impossibility of visibly discerning one drop of black blood, "concern about people passing as white became so great that even behaving like blacks or willingly associating with them were often treated as more important than any proof of actual black ancestry."[54] As Mencke points out, white Americans' desire for certitude surfaced in the literature of the period. Many novels written at this time betrayed public anxieties by employing the plot device of the tragedy of a white person discovering that he or she has black blood. This would often occur just before they were about to marry, forcing the wedding plans to be canceled.[55] The frequency with which these revelations occurred immediately before the individual was to be wed highlights anxiety over ensuring racially pure reproduction. These novels reflected a widespread obsession with racial purity and surety and gave voice to fears of passing, as well as doubts and fears about one's own racial status. As the desire for certitude increased, so did support for the one-drop rule, and by 1925, whites, blacks, and mulattoes, throughout both the North and South, were committed to the one-drop rule.[56]

The maintenance of white privilege and racial segregation was accomplished through the regulation of interracial sexuality. The Jim Crow system was characterized by the vigilant guarding of "white womanhood," even as it was common to assume "that a white boy doesn't become a man until he has had sexual relations with a black girl."[57] While it was considered a tragedy for a white woman to give birth to a mulatto child, it was insignificant to the white community if a black woman gave birth to a mulatto child, despite the fact that both cases involved the mixing of the races. F. James Davis suggests that this seeming paradox relies upon the assumption that children stay with their mothers, so the child will be defined as black if the mother is black. If the mother of a mulatto were white, however, the family, and the entire system of white dominance, would be threatened with "mongrelization."

> The supposed inferiority of the mixed child, according to the racist ideology, posed no threat so long as the white population remained "pure." . . . Here we see why the Jim Crow system required the continuation and strengthening of the one-drop rule for defining who is black, and why there was such complete opposition to the fall of the entire system.[58]

Fears of black political and economic equality were rearticulated as fears of interracial sexuality and black male sexuality. Sociologist Gunnar Myrdal confirmed this in his landmark study of white Americans' "rank order of discriminations."[59] Myrdal found that the greatest discrimination was expressed against the most intimate relations, listed below in order of decreasing intensity:

1. interracial marriage and sexual relations between black men and white women;
2. personal relations between blacks and whites, including talking or eating together, as well as dating;
3. sharing public facilities;
4. political participation;
5. equality in the legal system;
6. economic activity, including employment and public assistance.[60]

Subsequent research by sociologist Emory S. Bogardus confirmed that the white community was least accepting of interracial sexual relations.[61] Ironically, Myrdal also found that black Americans' resistance to discrimination was exactly the opposite: they were most interested in obtaining economic, legal, and political equality, and least desired interracial marriage and sexual contacts.[62] Whites most feared interracial sexual relations and assumed that increased political and economic freedom for blacks would necessarily lead down this path. F. James Davis notes that historically, whenever any change occurred in the four latter areas of discrimination, the white community responded with fear and accusations that black males were a threat to white womanhood. For example, emancipation, voting rights, and black competition with whites for jobs have all led to white violence aimed at blacks in the name of protecting white womanhood, and warding off the threat of interracial sexuality.[63]

Accordingly, when the 1954 *Brown v. Board of Education* decision was handed down by the United States Supreme Court, and the Jim Crow system was threatened, cries against miscegenation again rang loud. Arguments against desegregation throughout the 1950s and 1960s raised the banner of protecting white womanhood, warning that racial integration would inevitably lead to interracial sexuality and miscegenation. In his book *Black Monday*, Mississippi Circuit Court Judge Thomas Brady voiced these fears, threatening that the Supreme Court ruling in *Brown* would result in "the tragedy of miscegenation."[64] Every form of political and economic equality for blacks was depicted as a threat to white racial purity, responded to with fears of interracial sexuality, and argued against on this basis.

As the legal grounds for segregation crumbled, the Supreme Court declared in 1967 that states could no longer prohibit interracial marriage. Prior to that ruling, twenty-two states still had antimiscegenation statutes in place.[65] It was not until the early 1970s that Southern schools and other public facilities were finally forced to desegregate, and the South experienced tremendous change in race relations. While white acceptance of desegregated facilities progressed, approval of interracial dating and marriage did not. Despite widespread fears to the contrary, "miscegenation in the South seems to have been affected very little by the fall of the Jim Crow system and other successes of the Civil Rights movement."[66] While whites continued to refuse to accept blacks on a level of equality in close, especially sexual, relationships, black opposition to interracial sexuality increased during the 1960s and 1970s with the growth of the black pride movement. While the rate of black–white intermarriage increased 63 percent between

1960 and 1970, such marriages consistently represent only 1 to 2 percent of all marriages.[67]

Throughout the history of racial classification in the West, miscegenation and interracial sexuality have occupied a place of central importance. The science of racial differences has always displayed a preoccupation with the risks of interracial sexuality. Popular and legal discourses on race have been preoccupied with maintaining racial boundaries, frequently with great violence. This chapter suggests that racial classification, the maintenance of racial boundaries, and racism are inexorably linked. The construction of biological races and the belief in maintaining the hierarchy and separation of races has led to widespread fears of integration and interracial sexuality. Throughout U.S. history, the fear of black political and economic equality has been rearticulated as the fear of interracial sexuality and guarded against with force.

Additionally, gender has been central to this fear, as the protection of white womanhood and the threat of interracial sexuality have become synonymous. While interracial sexuality has been condemned historically, it has only been the relationship between white women and black men that has been the focus of attention; the exploitive relations between white men and black women have largely been ignored by the white community. The construction of whiteness as racially pure, and the enforcement of the one-drop rule, provided white males with the freedom to engage in interracial sexual relations, often through the rape of black women, while at the same time defending white womanhood against the fictional black male rapist. The myth of black sexuality as animal-like and out of control has served to justify the myth of the black male rapist and the institution of lynching. Additionally, for the white community, this myth has erased from view white males' sexual abuse of black women, who were defined as sexual creatures and therefore incapable of being raped. Defining black women as promiscuous and oversexed, combined with the belief that all women were the property of white men, meant that the only form of rape that was actually considered such was the rape of white women by black men. In this case, rape is seen as a violation of white male property rights. The intersections of race and gender are revealed in the entrenched paradox that while interracial sexuality has been condemned, it is only the relations between white women and black men that have been considered a threat to the white community.

Racial classification is essential to the preservation of white, and especially male, power and privilege. As this chapter highlights, racism is often a method of maintaining racial classification, and racial classification serves to support racism. As West argues, the

> basis for the idea of white supremacy is to be found in the classificatory categories and the descriptive, representational, order-imposing aims of natural history . . . the genealogy of racism in the modern West is inseparable from the appearance of the classificatory category of race.[68]

The history of racial classification, and beliefs about race and interracial sexuality, can be characterized as inherently white supremacist. White supremacy has been the law and prevailing worldview throughout U.S. history, and the ideology of what is today labeled the white supremacist movement is firmly rooted in this tradition. Accounts that label the contemporary white supremacist movement as fringe and extremist often have the consequence of rendering this history invisible. Understanding this history, however, is essential to understanding and combating both contemporary white supremacist and mainstream racism. Accounts that fail to address the important link between the U.S. history of white supremacist thought and contemporary white supremacism will prevent us from comprehending the strength and appeal of the contemporary movement while minimizing the centrality of racism to American history and identity. While a great deal has changed over the past three decades, the one-drop rule is still generally accepted, and interracial unions remain controversial and uncommon. As we shall see, contemporary white supremacist discourse rearticulates these white fears.

NOTES

1. Jordan 1969.
2. Banton and Harwood 1975, 14; Mencke 1979, 37.
3. Smedley 1993, 39.
4. Banton and Harwood 1975, 19.
5. Banton and Harwood 1975, 24.
6. West 1982, 55.
7. West 1982.
8. West 1982, 56.
9. Smedley 1993, 166.

10. West 1982, 54.
11. Young 1995.
12. Banton and Harwood 1975, 28.
13. Banton and Harwood 1975, 30.
14. Gould 1981, 46.
15. Gould 1981, 48.
16. Gould 1981, 49.
17. Gould 1981, 54.
18. Young 1995, 11.
19. Banton and Harwood 1975, 28.
20. Mencke 1979, 37–38.
21. Mencke 1979, 54.
22. Cope 1890, 2054 quoted in Mencke 1979, 57.
23. Shanklin 1994.
24. Mencke 1979, 46–47.
25. Mencke 1979, 48.
26. Shanklin 1994.
27. Collins, Wainer, and Bremner 1981, 14.
28. Hernstein and Murray 1994.
29. Young 1995, 94.
30. Young 1995, 19.
31. Davis 1991, 33; Giddings 1984, 37.
32. Giddings 1984, 37.
33. Davis 1991, 33.
34. Davis 1991, 34.
35. Davis 1983, 175.
36. Davis 1983; Davis 1991.
37. Mencke 1979, 8.
38. Mencke 1979, 22.
39. Davis 1991; Mencke 1979; Williamson 1980.
40. Mencke 1979, 18.
41. Davis 1991, 43.
42. Williamson 1980, 88–91.
43. Dixon 1902 in Mencke 1979, 210.
44. Mencke 1979, 37.
45. Dowd Hall 1992, 398.
46. Davis 1991, 52–53; Ware 1992, 181.
47. Davis 1983, 184.

48. Davis 1983, 185.
49. Carby 1986, 308.
50. Carby 1986, 308.
51. Carby 1986, 309.
52. Carby 1986, 309.
53. Davis 1991, 54.
54. Davis 1991, 56.
55. Mencke 1979.
56. Mencke 1979, 199.
57. Davis 1991, 62.
58. Davis 1991, 62.
59. Myrdal 1944, 60–61.
60. Myrdal 1944, 60–61.
61. Bogardus 1968, 149–52; Davis 1991, 60.
62. Davis 1991, 61; Myrdal 1944, 60–61.
63. Davis 1983; Davis 1991, 65.
64. Davis 1991, 17.
65. Davis 1991, 68.
66. Davis 1991, 70.
67. Davis 1991, 72–73.
68. West 1982, 55.

CULTIVATING THE SEED

The Organized White Supremacist Movement in the United States

> He don't believe in mixed relationships, that's just his opinion . . . it was okay for him to have black friends, and hang with black guys, but when mom brought home a black boyfriend that was not okay.[1]

This white woman appeared on a recent episode of *Sally Jessie Raphael*, distraught because her son had "disowned" her for her involvement in an interracial relationship. Her son defended his position, arguing,

> You can be friends with them but you don't sleep with them, you don't marry them. . . . I feel disgusted. She's ruined my name. I don't want my daughter thinking it's okay.[2]

Almost every week interracial relationships are the subject matter of a television talk show. Guests usually include white families upset over female family members' decision to date persons out of their race, most often black men. While audience members often chastise the guests' racism, these episodes clearly highlight an entrenched fear. Like the son on the aforementioned episode, many white Americans believe that while it may be acceptable to have friends of various races, it is not acceptable for a family member to date or marry out of their race.

Michael Eric Dyson observes that interracial sexuality remains a hotly contested subject among both white and black men and women. Interracial sexuality remains one of the remaining taboos of race and sex in our nation. . . . When a black man marries a white woman, it irks KKK types ("he's spoiled one of *our* women"); grieves many black mothers ("when a black son brings home a white woman, it's an insult to his mama"); angers many white men ("she's throwing her life away"); disappoints many black women ("with all these single black women, why would he choose a white woman?"); unnerves some white women ("I could never see myself with a black man"); and raises some black men's ire ("why do all these brothers, when they become sucessful, have to marry a white woman?"). This small sample of anecdotal responses to interracial relationships provides a glimpse of the furious passions and unresolved conflicts that continue to haunt love in black and white.[3]

With the exception of television talk shows, opposition to interracial relationships is often not voiced in public. White supremacist publications, however, forcefully and consistently argue against them. I find the very same threats underlying both white supremacist and mainstream white fears. At the core of this anxiety over interracial sexuality is the protection of racial and gender identity and privilege, highlighting the relationship between racism and the construction and maintenance of racial classifications.

Analyzing white supremacist discourse allows me to explore the varied ways in which racialized, gendered meanings are negotiated in discourse on interracial sexuality. Throughout this book, I examine white supremacist publications from the Keith Stimely collection, in the special collections of the University of Oregon's Knight Library (for a complete list of publications, see the appendix). This collection was the private collection of Stimely, who donated his holdings to the library. The collection contains the newsletters of a wide variety of white supremacist organizations, as well as miscellaneous paraphernalia, including flyers, leaflets, and membership materials from various organizations. The material I examined was published between 1969 and 1993. I examined all of the publications contained within the collection in order to ensure that I covered a wide range of organizations, with differing ideological frameworks and targeting different audiences. The collection is comprehensive, containing the publications of the largest organizations as well as very rare and obscure materials.

Each day, sequestered in the special collections room of the library where I was allowed to view these publications, was like entering another world. I faced a new language to learn and a basic underlying system of taken for granted assumptions so different from my own that it took many weeks before the discourse began to "make sense" to me. While many of the newsletters and magazines expressed divergent views on important issues, they all operated within a single framework for understanding racial and gender difference. Despite their differences, the various organizations share common ideologies and goals and an overriding commitment to maintaining white supremacy. While there are ongoing debates among the groups, there are also sustained efforts to forge shared objectives. For example, a 1992 issue of *NSV Report* entitled "Parallels: National Socialism & Identity Christianity" explains that

> Aside from some differences, there are many parallels between National Socialism and Identity Christianity that overshadow the differences, and the two belief systems go hand-in-hand. National Socialists and Identity Christians all believe in total geographic separation of all races and are White Nationalists, meaning they all want an all-White nation. Almost all White Nationalists believe in capital punishment for rapists, child molesters, homosexuals and racial miscegenators . . . the two belief systems actually complement each other.[4]

As this article suggests, the various branches of the contemporary white supremacist movement have a great deal in common. As Raphael S. Ezekiel found in his study of members of the movement, "the agreement on basic ideas is the glue that holds the movement together . . . the ideas are important to the members. The white racist movement is about an idea."[5] In terms of the focus of this study, the ideas are remarkably similar: the various groups share the belief that races are essentially and eternally different, believe in the necessity of keeping the races separate, and believe that miscegenation is the "ultimate abomination."

Because of the similarities and shared concerns of these organizations, there is a great deal of overlap in their memberships.[6] Divisions within the white supremacist movement often have more to do with personality differences and clashes than with divergences in belief and ideology.[7] It is also common to find that organizations support and distribute membership information and publications of other organizations. For instance, Western Guard America sends subscribers free samples of the National States Rights Party's *The Thunderbolt* and the National Alliance's *National Vanguard*.[8] Additionally, some of the publications examined here are not published by groups with memberships. For example, Western Guard America does "not function as a member-gathering organization but . . . attempt[s] to influence other patriotic organizations as for [*sic*] as policy making goes."[9] Similarly, *Instauration* is not an organizational newsletter, but a magazine read by members of various organizations.

HISTORY OF THE WHITE SUPREMACIST MOVEMENT

The organizations whose writings I examine represent the range of contemporary white supremacist thought. Historically, the white supremacist movement in the United States has been dominated by the Ku Klux Klan; however, the contemporary movement contains a variety of hybrid organizations drawing and expanding upon four varieties of white supremacist thought: the Ku Klux Klan, the neo-Nazis, the Christian Identity Church movement, and the militia movement. While there are many excellent studies that provide an in-depth look into these movements,[10] a brief overview will contribute to our understanding of the contemporary movement.[11]

The Ku Klux Klan

The Ku Klux Klan, historically the most influential white supremacist organization in the United States, was founded in Pulaski, Tennessee, in 1865, as a secret fraternal order for Civil War veterans of the confederate states. The Klan developed into a political organization with thousands of members who feared emancipated blacks as well as Northern carpetbaggers. At a convention in 1867 to unify the various dens that had been established, it was affirmed that " 'maintenance of the supremacy of the White Race in this Republic' was the 'main and fundamental objective' " of the Klan, and members had to pledge to oppose " 'social and political equality for Negroes.' "[12] The Klan led a reign of terror between 1867 and 1871, murdering, whipping, and torturing thousands of blacks. With the institutionalization of Jim Crow segregation, and the accompanying security of white domination, the Klan temporarily disbanded. After their dissolution, it became widely believed that the Klan had saved the South "from the perils of Reconstruction,"[13] and the Klan was glorified and romanticized in accounts such as Thomas Dixon's novel *The Clansman* (1905) and the subsequent film *Birth of a Nation* (1915).

The Klan reemerged in 1915, expanding its membership and gaining renewed respectability. Membership increased from five thousand in 1920 to between four and five million in 1925. Membership was a national phenomenon, included both men and women, and was especially popular among white Protestants. Members were often community leaders and, on the whole, represented the general population in terms of income, education level, and occupation.[14] Approximately five hundred thousand women were members of the women's auxiliary, Women of the Ku Klux Klan.[15]

The second Klan incorporated anti-Semitic, anti-Catholic, and anti-foreigner beliefs into its antiblack platform. The Klan's popularity was fueled by nativist sentiments opposed to the increased immigration rates of the past few decades, the migration of blacks to the North, increased ethnic intolerance, and fundamentalist beliefs. Amidst rapid social change, the Klan became a symbol of tradition and order.[16] As Leonard J. Moore suggests, the Klan articulated a "white Protestant ethnic identity."[17] The second Klan was transformed by publicity agents into a multimillion-dollar enterprise, exerting a strong influence on American politics.

By 1927, Klan membership declined to approximately three hundred fifty thousand. This decline was due to a number of factors, including the public's growing opposition to Klan violence, internal fighting among Klan leaders, and a number of financial scandals.[18] Moore, however, has suggested that the decline was also due in part to the elections won by various members of the Klan in the late 1920s that reaffirmed white, Protestant dominance and provided security in the belief that "deeply held traditional values, a common ethnic bond, and a sense of community seemed to have been upheld. Men and women who had believed that the foundation of their way of life might be crumbling beneath their feet" were once again comforted.[19]

The history of the second wave of the Klan challenges the widely held assumption that white supremacist movements thrive primarily in periods of difficult economic conditions. The Klan's resurgence in the 1920s occurred at a time of economic growth, while the decline coincided with the Great Depression, precisely the reverse of what one might expect, demonstrating that "Klan fortunes have been far more related to disruptive changes in societal conditions and institutions"[20] than simple economic distress.

Throughout the 1930s and early 1940s, reports of Klan violence continued, and communism and organized labor were added to its list of enemies.
The civil rights movements of the 1950s and 1960s triggered the next wave
of increased interest in the Klan. Following the 1954 United States Supreme
Court decision in *Brown v. Board of Education*, white opposition to desegregation led to vocal and violent opposition. New Klan groups increased in
strength, attracting Southern segregationists. Spearheading "the resistance
to a national trend toward equality for all Americans," Klan activity was
responsible for widespread violence against blacks and civil rights workers
throughout the 1960s.[21] Klan groups attracted between fifty-five and sixty-
five thousand members by 1965, and various Klan organizations competed
for membership.[22] While membership continued to increase amidst the riots
of the late 60s, it remained lower than one might expect given the historical
context. Offering an explanation for this seeming paradox, an ADL report
suggests that

> the Klans might have tapped the limits of their membership potential
> at that time, and that the white backlash triggered by the riots might
> have been so widespread and out in the open that angry whites no
> longer needed to join "secret" anti-black organizations.[23]

A congressional investigation and report in 1967 highlighting financial
mismanagement and terrorism, the imprisonment of a number of Klan leaders, and the decline in the civil rights movement led to a setback in Klan
membership in the late 1960s.[24] By 1973, membership declined to five thousand. Between 1973 and 1981, membership climbed back up to approximately eleven thousand five hundred. The Anti-Defamation League
attributes the increase in interest in the Klan in the late 1970s to "America's
frustrating defeat in Vietnam; a rising inflation rate; a costly and debilitating
dependence on foreign countries for crucial supplies of oil; and a backlash
against the atmosphere of social change and institutional challenge."[25] After
1981, Klan membership began a gradual decline to approximately four thousand in 1991, where it has remained since. This decline has been attributed
to a number of factors: newer white supremacist groups have sprung up,
attracting many Klan members and key figures, and numerous Klan members were implicated in, and convicted of, violent crimes.[26]

The Knights of the Ku Klux Klan, led by Thom Robb, is the largest,
most active contemporary Klan group. Robb has urged followers to abandon
overtly racist language in order to attract more members, suggesting that

the Klan is not about hate, but "love of the white race."[27] However, beneath this kinder, gentler facade, Robb draws upon the racist, anti-Semitic Identity doctrine (described below), and has proclaimed, "I hate Jews. I hate race-mixing Jews. We've let anti-Christ Jews into our country and we've been cursed with abortion, inflation, homosexuality and the threat of war."[28]

The Neo-Nazis

The American Nazi Party was founded in 1958 by George Lincoln Rockwell. Honoring the legacy of Hitler and the German Nazis, the American Nazi Party never gained many members. In contrast with the Ku Klux Klan's long history, grounded in mainstream politics in the United States,

> Rockwell's neo-Nazi movement brought an alien form to American extremism. . . . The American nation had gone to war to defeat Nazism. . . . For Americans, Rockwell's slogan of "White Power" was inextricably linked with memories of Nazism's genocidal past.[29]

Consequently, the American Nazi Party had only a few hundred supporters. However, Rockwell was an active and vocal leader who gained much publicity speaking across the country, targeting college campuses.

After Rockwell's assassination by a former party member, the party was in disarray. Matt Koehl, a founder of the National States' Rights Party in 1958, assumed leadership of the ANP in 1967. The party was renamed the National Socialist White People's Party, and "its goal remained the establishment of a Nazi-style regime in the United States."[30] Throughout the 1970s, the party experienced leadership conflicts and spawned numerous splinter groups. The ADL estimates that the combined membership of all neo-Nazi organizations in the United States totaled under 500 in 1984 and less than 450 by 1988, as members increasingly moved into the Klan and other white supremacist organizations.

In 1983 the NSWPP was restructured and renamed the New Order. The New Order has been one of the strongest and most stable neo-Nazi organizations in recent years. Still under the leadership of Koehl, this organization remains the most strictly committed to Nazi ideals and maintains international contacts through the World Union of National Socialists. In 1988, the New Order had about twenty-five hard-core activists and one hundred official members, dedicated to the "fulfillment of Adolf Hitler's great mission."[31]

The second most active neo-Nazi organization is the National Alliance, formerly the National Youth Alliance, headed by a former Oregon State University physics professor and longtime Nazi activist, William Pierce. Under the pseudonym Andrew Macdonald, Pierce wrote the white supremacist utopian novel *The Turner Diaries* (identified as the blueprint for the 1995 Oklahoma City bombing).

Neo-Nazi Skinheads are perhaps the most violent wing of the white supremacist movement today, with over seventy thousand youths active in thirty-three countries linked by traveling Skinhead rock bands and their recordings, a variety of publications known as skinzines, and, increasingly, through the Internet. Skinhead gangs of teenagers are often highly visible, with closely shaven heads, combat boots, bomber jackets, thin suspenders, and Nazi tatoos. Skinhead groups may vary in size from a handful to a few dozen members. Skinheads have been responsible for dozens of murders, including those of a policeman and an African national in two separate incidents in Denver in 1997.

Music is the recruitment tool of choice for Skinheads. Through white power "oi" music, Skinheads attract youngsters searching for meaning and community. Skinhead youths often come from unstable families, and Skinhead groups often function as surrogate families.[32] Through music, they maintain international connections, and unite on concert tours and at music festivals. "Oi" music, by bands such as Skrewdriver and Bound For Glory, sport racist lyrics and violent imagery on jacket artwork. Resistance Records in Detroit is a popular producer of Skinhead music and publishes a magazine with a self-proclaimed circulation of over twelve thousand. The words of a song by Skinhead band Nordic Thunder is typical of the Skinhead racist, anti-Semitic message: "I know the truth and I know what is right. To destroy the zionist way and keep my land White. . . . I've sworn to protect my people, For that I am crucified, I live for my Race and for my Race I will die."[33]

Skinhead factions have been growing at the same time as more traditional white supremacist groups have experienced a decline. Skinheads first appeared in the United States in the early 1980s and have since sprouted in at least forty states. Their overt presence and unrestrained violence have reenergized the movement. They rely upon their boots, bats, knives, and guns to terrorize and murder minorities, interracial couples, homosexuals, nonracist Skinheads, and the homeless and have been charged with other crimes, including planning to bomb an African American church in California and bombing an NAACP office and a gay bar in Washington.[34]

While there is no unified Skinhead organization throughout the United States, Skinheads are integrated into the larger white supremacist movement, primarily through their relationships with mentors. Mentors like Tom Metzger and Gary Lauck instruct Skinheads in white supremacist ideology, supply them with written propaganda and include them in other white supremacist gatherings and conventions. Skinheads frequently march with Klan groups and regularly attend youth gatherings at the Aryan Nations compound.

Many Skinheads are rejecting the traditional Skinhead garb in order to make themselves less conspicous to law enforcement agents. However, it is also important to note that not all Skinheads are racist. In fact, other Skinheads, like the SHARPS (Skinheads Against Racial Prejudice), are increasingly defining themselves as "antiracist" Skinheads, in order not only to distinguish themselves from the racist Skinheads, but to take an active stance against racism.[35] Consequently, they have at times been the victims of racist Skinhead violence.

The Christian Identity Church Movement

The Christian Identity Church movement was not recognized as a strong presence within the white supremacist movement until the 1970s and early 1980s. The racist and anti-Semitic Identity doctrine provides the theological underpinnings for a variety of white supremacist organizations and links various groups together.

Rev. Wesley Swift was a leading early proponent of Identity doctrine in the 1940s and 1950s. A one-time Ku Klux Klan leader, Swift led a California Identity church called the Anglo-Saxon Christian Congregation. The Aryan Nations' leader, Richard Butler, today leads the Church of Jesus Christ Christian, the Identity church that considers itself the successor to Swift's Identity congregation.[36]

Aryan Nations is a paramilitary organization with several hundred followers. At their compound in Hayden Lake, Idaho, they host a "World Congress," as well as youth gatherings each year, drawing together white supremacists from numerous organizations throughout the world, especially attracting young Skinheads. A virulently anti-Semitic organization, it seeks to establish a white homeland in the Northwest.

Another significant Identity church group is the Posse Comitatus, a survivalist group founded by William P. Gale. Thom Robb, Grand Wizard of the Knights of the Ku Klux Klan and editor of *The Torch* and *The White Patriot* (both discussed here), is also a leading Identity movement figure.

Identity doctrine has its foundations in British Israelism of the mid-1800s. As Leonard Zeskind explains, "It is no accident that a religious movement based on racial lineage developed in the mid-nineteenth century. Racism was developing a 'scientific' cast at that time."[37] British Israelism drew upon scientific studies of race and was influenced by the burgeoning eugenics movement. The aversion to interracial sexuality found throughout racial discourse at the time became a prominent feature of British Israelism and Identity doctrine. Based on an "idiosyncratic reading" of the Bible, British Israelism holds that the people of Israel settled in northern Europe before the Christian era. According to the Bible, ancient Israel was divided into two kingdoms: the northern portion consisted of ten of the twelve tribes descended from Jacob, and when the area was conquered the ten tribes were lost. The Jews of today are supposedly descendants of the southern kingdom, but according to Identity belief

> characteristics of the racial type we recognize as that of the Jews today were the result of intermarriages in the days of Ezra and Nehemiah. At that time a mutation of the blood stream occurred . . . a defection from God's will.[38]

This racialization of biblical beliefs recasts the ancient Hebrews as a race, whose descendants today are the Aryans, and deems Jews the product of race-mixing.[39]

American theologians have contributed to Identity doctrine, adding the "two seed" theory.[40] U.S. Identity doctrine holds that there were two creations: the first was the male and female created in Genesis 1:26–27, and the second was Adam and Eve in Genesis 2:2–6. These two accounts supposedly produced two separate races, reminiscent of nineteenth-century theories of polygenesis. Adam is the ancestor of the Caucasian race today, and the other male and female produced the pre-Adamic "mud people," people without souls, considered today's blacks and other non-Jewish nonwhites. According to Identity doctrine, Satan seduced Eve, and Eve introduced sexual intercourse to Adam. Eve was impregnated with two seeds, Satan's evil seed, producing Cain, and God's, producing Abel. When Cain, the evil one, was cast out of Eden, he supposedly married a pre-Adamic woman, leading to the Jewish race. According to this account, Jews are not only the children of Satan, but once again the product of racial intermixture.[41]

This racialization of the Bible also provides the Identity movement with a racial destiny. According to this doctrine, it is the destiny of the Anglo-Saxons to establish God's kingdom on earth, and the United States and Great Britain are considered their birthright, the blessings of Joseph promised in the Bible. Their "birthright is to be the wealthiest, most powerful nations on earth . . . able, by divine right, to dominate and colonize the world."[42] According to Identity doctrine, white Anglo-Saxons are the descendants of the ten lost tribes and are the Bible's chosen people, and the United States and England are the true Israel. According to Identity belief, Jesus was not Jewish, but Northern European, and the second coming of Christ is not far off. The second coming will be heralded by a great cataclysm—economic and political chaos, widespread destruction, and cities in flames as a result of a race war, and only Identity followers will survive and build the true Israel in America.[43]

Militia Movement[44]

Since the first militias began appearing in 1994, their numbers have expanded to include fifteen thousand members in at least forty states. Militias charge that the federal government is eroding our constitutional rights and establish common-law courts, self-appointed vigilante groups that usurp the authority of the law. They declare themselves exempt from state and federal law and reserve the right to arrest and murder the opposition. While the militia movement is not as overtly racist and anti-Semitic as the above white supremacist organizations, Morris Dees and Robert Crawford and Devin Burghart argue it is "a tool for furthering the white supremacist struggle for the erection of a white Christian republic on U.S. soil."[45] While some militias have consciously distanced themselves from racist ties, others constitute a virtual alternative government representing the interests of white supremacists. Militias are the direct descendants of the Posse Comitatus, a group of activists who embrace Christian Identity doctrine, and join it with an antigovernment agenda. The Christian Patriots, the modern-day descendants of the Posse Comitatus, have led the effort to establish both militias and common-law courts. Refusing to pay taxes, counterfeiting money, and stockpiling weapons, they recognize the county sheriff as the only legal law enforcement officer.[46] The most frequent form of militia racism is rooted in the Christian Patriot notion that the true Constitution protects only whites and their refusal to recognize the Thirteenth and Fourteenth Amendments. "The 'We the People' referred to in the Constitution, they write, refers to 'the white race and none other.' "[47] Dees and Crawford and Burghart demonstrate, convincingly, that the militias "are informed by a legacy of bigotry . . . [the] latest tool of the far right."[48]

The Contemporary White Supremacist Movement

The contemporary movement is diverse and these four strands have contributed to the proliferation of new hybrid organizations. Responding to the movements for racial, gender, and sexual equality that blossomed in the 1960s, the contemporary movement can be characterized as a backlash. As Michael Omi explains, the civil rights movement and the subsequent shift in racial politics

> ushered in a period of desegregation efforts, "equal opportunity" mandates, and other state reforms. By the early seventies, however, a "backlash" could be discerned to the institutionalization of these reforms and to the political realignments set in motion in the 1960s.[49]

The white supremacist movement depicts these shifts as an attack on whites. Crime, immigration, integration, affirmative action, education: whatever is focused on is defined as part of a multipronged assault on whites. For example, an article in *White Patriot* asserts that "the White people of America have become an oppressed majority. Our people suffer from discrimination in the awarding of employment, promotions, scholarships, and college entrances."[50]

Much of supremacist discourse appropriates the rhetoric of the civil rights movement to defend the interests of whites. As the certainty of racial segregation broke down, white supremacist fears grew. As Zygmunt Bauman has observed, "As long as they are effective, practices of separation do not need the support of attitudinal hostility."[51] Once threatened, however, hostility increases. Bauman has found that historically racism and anti-Semitism have found greater expression during periods of great social upheaval, especially among those "about to be uprooted, disinherited and ploughed out of their secure social locations by the new social order which they could not but perceive as chaos."[52] The visible boundaries and borders separating and marking races have been threatened with disruption. As in the past, when secure boundaries separating races begin to break down, fears of racial intermixture and unknown racial heritage emerge.

Response to this shift has not been limited to extremist movements, however. For example, *The Report on Democratic Defection*, a study of traditional Democrats who voted Republican in 1980 and 1984, found that many young, white males blame blacks for the major problems they face in their lives. As one subject responded, "Everybody but the white male race gets advantages now."[53] Charles Gallagher found that backlash and anger characterize the current feelings of many white college students. He concludes that "many whites see themselves as victims of the multicultural, pc, feminist onslaught [and this] would be laughable if it were not for the sense of mental crisis and the reactionary backlash that underpin these beliefs."[54] Central to this backlash is a sense of confusion over the meaning of whiteness, triggered by the perceived loss of white privilege.[55] The contemporary white supremacist movement has been able to attract some of these disillusioned whites, primarily male, who now believe that their interests are not being represented. As Ezekiel suggests, "white rule in America has ended, members feel. A new world they do not like has pushed aside the traditional one they think they remember."[56]

Omi draws a comparison between the burgeoning white supremacist movement and the growing neoconservative project, which both attack the liberal racial policy of the 1960s and 1970s. Omi suggests that the

> far right is driven by white working class anger with the perceived demise of white skin privilege and the political and social empowerment of racial minorities in the post-Civil Rights era. Neoconservatism, by contrast, is an intellectual movement of elite academics who have attempted to create a new political and policy-making consensus.[57]

However, despite commonly held assumptions that white supremacists are uneducated or especially hard-hit victims of economic upheaval, research confirms that, like earlier incarnations of the Klan, contemporary white supremacist group members are similar to the U.S. population in general in terms of education, income, and occupation.[58] Additionally, there are white supremacist periodicals that are produced by, and specifically target, highly educated audiences (especially *Instauration*, reviewed here).

While somewhat diverse in terms of class and education, the diversity ends there. White supremacist discourse is a masculine enterprise. White men are the writers, publishers, and editors of the publications, and they occupy central roles within the pages of the publications.[59] While the contemporary white supremacist movement is concerned with rearticulating a white identity in response to the challenges of racial and ethnic social movements, this white identity is most certainly a gendered identity. Gender is often an overlooked dimension of analyses and reports on the movement, yet gender issues share center stage in the publications. The contemporary white supremacist movement clearly responds to the second wave of the feminist movement and the growing gay and lesbian movement and the challenges these have presented to traditional gender and sexual identities. Susan Faludi has documented the breadth of this backlash, ranging from film and television portrayals to the growth of a reactionary men's movement. Certainly, the white supremacist movement comprises only one small part of this broad-based backlash. As Michael S. Kimmel observes, the fact "That men are today confused about what it means to be a 'real man'—that masculinity is in crisis—has become a cultural commonplace."[60] Responding to what is perceived as a threat to both racial and gendered certainties, the contemporary white supremacist movement is primarily preoccupied with rearticulating white male identity and privilege.[61]

Analyses have traditionally focused on men in the movement, and historically men have formed the bulk of the membership.[62] Nevertheless, gender issues are central to comprehending this male-centered discourse. Ezekiel notes that the organizations he observed remain almost exclusively male, and work within the organizations is strictly segregated by gender. He notes, "a few women are around, never as speakers or leaders; usually they are wives, who cook and listen. Highly traditional ideas of sex roles, and fears of losing male dominance, fill the conversation and speeches."[63] Kathleen Blee's recent work on the contemporary movement, however, documents the efforts of many organizations to recruit women into their ranks. Why are these organizations targeting women? One Southern Klan leader's description of his rationale for pursuing women recruits is typical:

> In order to bring in the men, the men will follow the women. If a wife is against the husband's being involved, you can just about . . . forget

the husband hanging around for long. . . . The other way, if the wife is into it, she'll drag the husband along.[64]

Women have been targeted for recruitment by various organizations as a strategy to increase and stabilize membership by bringing entire families into the fold. Figures 1a and 1b depict the efforts of Glen Miller's *White Patriot Party* to recruit women and families, which were featured in an issue of *The Spotlight*.[65] "As a result," Blee suggests, "women now play a highly visible and significant role in the racist movement, constituting about 25 percent of the membership (and nearly 50 percent of the new recruits) in some Klan and neo-Nazi groups."[66] I suspect that the divergent accounts of women's involvement suggest that women's participation in the movement is uneven and largely dependent upon the recruitment efforts of specific organizations. As we will see, however, the discourse of the white supremacist movement remains highly gendered, and it will be important for future analyses to explore if and how this discourse changes in response to the growing numbers of women in these organizations.

Since the early 1970s, a wide range of radical white supremacist organizations have been founded. The Intelligence Project of the Southern Poverty Law Center, established to monitor hate group activity, identified 462 white supremacist hate groups in existence throughout the United States in 1997.[67] This estimate does not include racist and anti-Semitic militia groups. It is difficult to estimate the membership of hate groups, which is often concealed. Ezekiel reports that hard-core members number twenty-three to twenty-five thousand.

While membership in white supremacist organizations declined throughout the 1980s, the movement became increasingly violent. The ADL observes that the years from 1982 to 1988 "have been among the more violent periods in the history of American hate groups."[68] Tracking organizations like the ADL have provided documentation of dozens of murders and attempted murders committed by Klan members, Skinheads, and other white supremacists, including an attempt to plant dynamite in a Jewish synagogue in Tennessee in May 1981; six Klansmen's attempt to invade the Caribbean island republic of Dominica and overthrow its government in April 1981; the firing of over one hundred rounds of ammunition into the offices of Mississippi's largest black newspaper in January 1982; and the breaking and shooting into of the homes of interracial families in Georgia and North Carolina, throughout 1984 and 1985.[69] Additionally, since the early 1980s, numerous organizations have established camps for paramilitary training, preparing members for deliberate acts of violence as well as the coming "race war." Throughout the 1980s, dozens of white supremacists have been convicted of murders, robberies, fire bombings, conspiracies to overthrow the government, and other such acts. Organizations have been found stockpiling weapons and bombs and planning actions designed to provoke a race war, including one group's intention to "poison the water supply of an unnamed city" with cyanide.[70] Certainly the bombing of the Oklahoma City Federal Building was the most deadly in this line of attack. Although certain arms of the movement have become increasingly violent, other white supremacists, including the well-publicized case of David Duke, have moved further into the mainstream, entering traditional American politics.

While hard-core membership in the movement is limited, far more people actually read the discourse. Approximately one hundred fifty thousand people purchase movement literature and take part in activities, and an additional four hundred fifty thousand read the movement literature, even though they do not purchase it themselves.[71] The ADL estimates that fifty white supremacist periodicals publish continuously.[72]

In addition to printed materials, white supremacists are increasingly turning to the Internet to spread their hate, through bulletin boards and World Wide Web sites like the Stormfront's *White Pride, World Wide* home page. The Internet is a valuable new tool in the white supremacist arsenal. It is easy, cheap, instantaneous, and highly accessible. It provides international connections and virtual anonymity for its participants and audience. Computer technology allows Web site designers to provide messages for the public, as well as secret messages that can only be accessed using code words, providing "an avenue of propagandizing among outsiders as well as a fairly secure message center for initiates."[73] Additionally, increasing numbers of people may now stumble upon white supremacist literature without having to seek it out. Traditional organizations like the Klan, the neo-Nazi National Alliance, and the Institute for Historical Review (a clearinghouse for Holocaust denial) have turned to the Internet and established Web sites. Additionally, however, new, young, amateurish groups and individuals have found the Web a hospitable medium for self-promotion. The ADL reports that there are at least two hundred and fifty "hate sites" on the Internet.[74]

Many studies of the white supremacist movement focus on active members and their motivations for joining the movement.[75] The number of these members is quite small, however, compared with the number of people who regularly read or encounter white supremacist discourse. For this reason it is important that we begin to focus more attention on the literature itself. Many researchers assume that participant observation or in-depth interviews are the most appropriate way to discover what attracts individuals to the movement. This type of research, while crucial, only sheds light on the motivations of the hard-core members of the movement; it tells us nothing of the over half a million readers of white supremacist literature who do not participate in white supremacist activity. I want to turn our attention to this literature so that we can begin to ask why so many people find it pleasurable or compelling.

Just as fears of miscegenation and the desire for scientific racial categorizations skyrocketed after emancipation, once again, as boundaries once assumed to be secure break down, the desire for racial surety has increased, at least among a segment of the population. The contemporary white supremacist movement embodies these fears, which manifest themselves, as among previous generations, "in the acute fear of the void, the never-satiated lust for certainty, paranoic mythologies of conspiracy and the frantic search for ever-elusive identity."[76]

NOTES

1. *Sally Jessie Raphael*, 18 December 1996.
2. *Sally Jessie Raphael*, 18 December 1986.
3. Dyson 1993, 228.
4. *The NSV Report* July/September 1992, 1.
5. Ezekiel 1995, xxix.
6. Anti-Defamation League 1988b, 1; Harper 1993; Langer 1990.
7. Harper 1993, 56.
8. *The Western Guardian* April 1980, 1.
9. *The Western Guardian* April 1980, 1.
10. Aho 1990; Anti-Defamation League 1988a, 1988b, 1995, 1996a; Blee 1991b, 1996; Chalmers 1965; Coates 1987; Dees 1996; Diamond 1995; Ezekiel 1995; George and Wilcox 1992; Katz 1987; Moore 1991; Ridgeway 1990; Sims 1978; Wade 1987; Zeskind 1986.
11. This outline is sketchy because I am more interested in situating white supremacist ideology within mainstream racial ideology. The goal of this

book is *not* to provide an in-depth picture of the organized hate movement itself.

12. Anti-Defamation League 1988b, 75.

13. Harper 1993, 33.

14. Harper 1993, 35; Blee 1991b; Moore 1991; Anti-Defamation League 1988b, 78.

15. Blee 1991b, 2.

16. Harper 1993, 37; Chalmers 1987; Lipset and Raab 1970; Moore 1991.

17. Moore 1991, 187.

18. Anti-Defamation League 1988b, 78; Blee 1991a, 72.

19. Moore 1991, 185.

20. Anti-Defamation League 1988b, 79.

21. Anti-Defamation League 1988b, 82.

22. Harper 1993, 41; Anti-Defamation League 1988b, 85.

23. Anti-Defamation League 1988b, 85.

24. Anti-Defamation League 1988b, 85.

25. Anti-Defamation League 1988b, 86.

26. Anti-Defamation League 1991, 1.

27. Anti-Defamation League 1996a.

28. Anti-Defamation League 1996a.

29. Anti-Defamation League 1988b, 24.

30. Anti-Defamation League 1988b, 25.

31. Anti-Defamation League 1988b, 26.

32. Anti-Defamation League 1995, 78.

33. Anti-Defamation League 1996a.

34. Anti-Defamation League 1995, 82.

35. Anti-Defamation League 1995, 82.

36. Anti-Defamation League 1988b, 40.

37. Zeskind 1986, 15.

38. Zeskind 1986, 196.

39. Barkun 1994.

40. Ridgeway 1990, 54.

41. Aho 1990; Anti-Defamation League 1988b; Barkun 1994.

42. Zeskind 1986, 19.

43. Anti-Defamation League 1988b, 40.

44. The militia movement is a recent phenomenon, and not included among the organizations whose publications I examined.

45. Crawford and Burghart 1997, 190; Dees 1996.

46. Crawford and Burghart 1997; Anti-Defamation League 1996a.
47. Crawford and Burghart 1997, 199.
48. Crawford and Burghart 1997, 200.
49. Omi 1991, 78.
50. *White Patriot* no. 56, 6.
51. Bauman 1989, 36.
52. Bauman 1989, 46.
53. Omi 1991, 79.
54. Gallagher 1995, 169.
55. Gallagher 1995; Steinberg 1995.
56. Ezekiel 1995, xxv.
57. Omi 1991, 80.
58. Aho 1990; Ezekiel 1995; Harper 1993.
59. Harper 1993.
60. Kimmel 1987, 121.
61. Daniels 1997; Ferber 1995b, 1998a.
62. However, Blee documents the involvement of women in the Klan of the 1920s. See Blee 1991a, 1991b.
63. Ezekiel 1995, xxvii.
64. Blee 1996, 682.
65. *The Spotlight* 20 January, 1986, 16.
66. Blee 1995, 1.
67. Intelligence Project of The Southern Poverty Law Center 1998, 6.
68. Anti-Defamation League 1988b, 1.
69. Anti-Defamation League 1988b, 11–5.
70. Anti-Defamation League 1988b, 71.
71. Ezekiel 1995; Harper 1993, 43.
72. Anti-Defamation League 1988b, 1.
73. Coates 1987, 207.
74. Roberts 1997.
75. Aho 1990; Blee 1991a, 1991b; Ezekiel 1995; Langer 1990; Ridgeway 1990; Zeskind 1986.
76. Bauman 1989, 46.

PART II

READING WHITE SUPREMACY

DEFINING DIFFERENCE

> Perhaps the cruelest hoax is the liberal lie of telling the Negro he's the equal of the White man and expecting to make an instant White man out of him by sending him to college, giving him a federal handout. . . . Let's have the honesty and decency to recognize the Negro for what he is, and not make impossible demands of him. . . . This has nothing to do with "hate" or "bigotry." I love my dog, for example, but I'm not about to recognize her as my equal.[1]

White supremacist discourse frequently ridicules feminists, antiracists, and others who fight for human equality. While equality is obviously a threat to white male privilege and power, white supremacists also perceive it as a threat to the existence of the white race itself. Affirmative action and integration are depicted as leading to white genocide. I suspect (and hope) that to most readers of this book this will sound ridiculous. This line of thinking only makes sense within the broader framework of the white supremacist worldview and, more specifically, within the equality versus difference opposition that grounds white supremacist logic.

Throughout white supremacist discourse, race and gender are constructed as differences, and because binary oppositions are always hierarchized, difference is equated with inequality. The other side of the opposition, equality, becomes equated with sameness. The difference/equality dichotomy recasts equality as necessarily requiring sameness, while difference necessarily requires and justifies hierarchy.

The difference/equality opposition is not limited to white supremacist discourse. For example, as Joan W. Scott suggests, this dichotomy has been used to characterize various schools of feminist thought, and it is also evident in debates about racial inequality. Historically, certain branches of the women's movement have argued that men and women are essentially the same and therefore deserve equal treatment. Another school of feminist thought has held that men and women are different and should be treated differently. This position, however, has been used to justify discrimination against women in the name of their different needs and desires, as happened in the *Sears* case, the sex discrimination suit waged by the Equal Employment Opportunity Commission in 1979, discussed by Scott in her article "Deconstructing Equality-Versus-Difference: Or, the Uses of Poststructuralist Theory for Feminism." In this case, it was assumed that if it could be shown that women actually are different from men, then unequal pay and job stratification could be justified. Scott suggests that

> Instead of framing analyses and strategies as if such binary pairs were timeless and true, we need to ask how the dichotomous pairing of equality and difference itself works . . . [to] understand how the concepts work to constrain and construct specific meanings.[2]

As Scott suggests, the difference/equality dichotomy makes certain meanings possible and others incomprehensible. Within this discursive framework, race and gender differences are constructed as necessarily hierarchical, so that any attempt to question inequality is represented as a threat to difference itself. All arguments in support of equality are defined as attempts to erase difference and make everyone the same. An equality that recognizes differences is impossible within this framework. The difference/equality opposition is central to white supremacist discourse, and an analysis of how this dichotomy works to construct meaning will allow us to both understand and call into question this system of (il)logic.

CONSTRUCTING RACIAL ESSENCE

While white supremacist discourse adamantly supports the notion that race is a biological and/or God-given essence, my review of the discourse reveals the social construction of that essence. Exploring this discourse reveals the construction of both race and gender as inner essences, immutable and natural.

Throughout white supremacist discourse, whiteness is defined in terms of visible, physical differences in appearance. According to one article, true whites are Nordics, "the thin, fair and symmetric race originating in Northern Europe."[3] In another article, Nordics are described as

> the only cleanly chiselled faces around. And there are other ways they stand out. The world's finest hair and finest skin texture are in Scandinavia. Some of the world's tallest statures, largest body size and most massive heads are also found in Northern European regions.[4]

Jews are also constructed as a race in this discourse, identifiable by physical markers such as "long kinky curls and typical hooked nose, thick fleshy lips, slant eyes and other typical Jew features."[5]

A number of periodicals rely upon an evolutionary framework, presenting evolution as a clear path of increasing racial differentiation. As a *New Order* article explains, "Race is everything because it is the Unit of Evolution, the genetic entity by which the Will-to-improvement is expressed and realized."[6] Evolution is also invoked to support racial inequality. For example, a *White Power* article explains that there is enough evidence to conclude that "the Negroid race is about 200,000 years less developed than either the White or Yellow races."[7]

Evolution is cast within the difference/equality framework to suggest that difference and its correlate, inequality, are facts of nature. An article in *Instauration* entitled "Evolution vs. Integration" emphasizes this, explaining,

> the Negro brain is only 10.6% smaller than a white's. But in regard to the more recently attained capacity for abstract and rational thought, the gap is much larger. . . . There is no underlying unity upon which to build or maintain a functioning social matrix.[8]

This article suggests that any attempt to integrate the races runs counter to the natural course of evolution and is bound to fail. Genetic difference and evolution, as the path of increasing differentiation, are constructed as rooted in nature, reifying inequality as a natural, permanent fact of life.

According to Christian Identity theology, discussed earlier, difference is destiny—it is God-given. Nonwhites are not simply biologically or genetically different from whites, they are also not considered God's children. They are defined as pre-Adamic mud people, not the offspring of Adam. As a *Thunderbolt* article proclaims, "the colored and mongrelized races do not have God's Spirit and cannot be accepted . . . [we] cannot change God's laws."[9]

A great deal of effort is put into physically distinguishing races from one another. Both the book and film entitled *Blood in the Face* take their name from some white supremacists' supposition that Jews cannot blush and only true whites show "blood in the face."[10] Rather than revealing race as a biological essence, this discourse reveals the continued effort required to construct racial differences, demonstrating Judith Butler's assertion that identities are constructed through reiterative and citational practices.[11] The construction of identity is not a singular act or gesture, but rather a process, or performance, as Butler calls it, which must be continually repeated. The elaboration of racial and sexual difference must *"repeat itself* in order to establish the illusion of its own uniformity and identity."[12]

The process of repetition that strives to construct race and gender as essential identities reveals their construction. These identities are always at risk and never secure. The endless repetition through which they are constructed suggests that they require this repetition for their existence; they are not given or self-evident. This point is important to my argument because it allows us actually to witness the process of construction within white supremacist writings.

Even though racial identity is posited as a biological or God-given fact of nature, the definition of whiteness is in constant flux. There is disagreement among groups and individuals over the characteristics that define whiteness and who is, or is not, white. In some of the discourse, Aryans are defined as strictly Northern Europeans, and there is debate over exactly where to draw the line in Europe. As one white supremacist claims in the film *Blood in the Face*, "we're more Nazi than the Nazis were!"

Because the visible characteristics constructed as markers of race are not always evident, discerning the race of individuals is of the utmost importance to white supremacists. Articles such as "Racial Tagging" in *Instauration* reveal surprises in the racial identity of public figures. As this article explains,

> Racial identification is a tricky game. As we keep our eyes open, we stumble across the most surprising information. Recently we have been looking into the Portuguese origins of public figures considered to have been solidly Northern European in racial makeup.[13]

Racial identity is constructed as an essence within each person that merely needs to be discovered, not unlike the approach of social scientists studying intermarriage. This discovery of race, however, is the *production* of the racialized subject.

References to the realness of race are the means through which race as a reality is constructed. The racialized body is posited as existing prior to its signification and outside of discourse, but the racialized body is an effect of discourse, produced through these reiterative and citational practices. Throughout this discourse, racial bodies are produced in a flood of articles and references to physical differences. Columns that catalogue physical differences appear frequently, like this typical feature in *Instauration* entitled "Racial Clues":

> Facial hair sprouts differently on blacks. . . . Different races have different enzymes which show up in their blood. . . . Whites have a more "angular" mouth roof than blacks, whose roofs have a horseshoe configuration. Also the nasal opening in the skull of blacks is larger than that of whites.[14]

White supremacist discourse gains the authority to construct race as an origin and essence partly through citational practices that invoke the authority of science, as in the above articles. Sociologist Steven Seidman suggests that the power of discourse to create normative conceptions of race derives from the extent to which it can invoke "the intellectual and social authority of science. A discourse that bears the stamp of scientific knowledge gives its normative concepts of identity and order an authority."[15] Throughout this discourse, the authority of science is invoked to support white supremacist propositions. Discussion of racial difference almost always includes references to names of scientists and doctors. For example, a rather typical article reports that

> Dr. Audrey Shuey of Northern Illinois University states that the average negro has an I.Q. 15 to 20 points lower than that of an average White individual. . . . Dr. Robert Gayre has conducted many studies which show that the negro brain is on the average 100 milligrams lighter than the White brain. . . . Dr. Carlton Putnam . . . says that the convolutions and thickness of the suprannual layer of the negro brain cortex is 14% thinner than the White's. . . . Professor Donald Swan of Hattiesburg University states that the difference between the races is up to 75% caused by heredity.[16]

Similarly, *Instauration* articles frequently not only cite but also provide in-depth discussions of the work of scientists and academicians in articles like one entitled "The Sociobiology Debate," which provides a discussion of the work of prominent sociobiologists.[17] Not surprisingly, white supremacy finds much support and confirmation of its arguments in sociobiology, highlighting the difficulty of drawing the line between who is or is not a white supremacist and demonstrating that the organized white supremacist movement continues to rely upon mainstream allies.

The reliance upon science is spotty, however. The only science deemed legitimate is that which supports their racist assumptions; all other science is dismissed as biased propaganda, the work of a liberal, Jewish elite. White supremacists assure themselves they know the Truth when they see it. According to this circular logic, whether or not research is valid depends on its conclusions—if it supports the white supremacist message, it is good, "objective" science.

While a great amount of effort and written space is devoted to delineating physical racial differences, these physical differences are always interpreted as signifying deeper, underlying differences. Physical differences produce the illusion of an inner racial essence. For example, the photographs in figure 2 were published in the *National Vanguard* to exaggerate racial differences. The photographs represent an African American girl, a white girl, and a Jewish girl, and the caption beneath them claims,

> ONLY THE FOOL or the mischief-maker can claim that the same soul dwells in the breast of the Negro, the White, and the Jew. Body and soul are interdependent, and the face more often than not reveals the essence of the inner nature.[18]

As this photograph and caption demonstrate, differences in intelligence, morality, character, and culture are all posited as racially determined. As an *NSV Report* article proclaims, "racists believe that values and ideals are a manifestation of race and are thus biologically inherited."[19] Mirroring the work of earlier generations of scientists and anthropologists, physical and cultural characteristics are linked, both assumed to be determined by race and therefore unchanging. Politics, music, art, and science are all shaped by race in this discourse. *The Thunderbolt* proclaims that

> The White Race has created and developed most of the world's present and past civilizations . . . responsible for almost all of the scientific, engineering and productive know-how that has raised the world's standard of living . . . the only race which has been able to maintain a

free democratic government. Liberty, justice and freedom only exist in White nations . . . [as do] culture, art, humanities. . . . The charity and goodness of the White Race have time and again saved the non-White peoples of the world from famine and plague. The White Race in the past has established moral codes, rules and laws, and educational systems for the advancement of society that have been unsurpassed by any other race in the world.[20]

Like conceptions of race developed in the eighteenth and nineteenth centuries, civilization is a marker for whiteness. Additionally, this racial essence is represented as immutable. An *NSV Report* article about Jews claims,

We fight for things that they cannot understand because of their nature; and because of their nature, they can never understand because they are aliens. Even if they changed their religion, they will not be a part of our Folk. They can never be a part of our Folk for they are aliens. They might as well be from another planet because they are not of our world.[21]

Regardless of the topic, the issue is overdetermined by racial meanings. Hair texture, skin color, criminal behavior, and the success of nations are all said to be determined by race. For example, crime is frequently presented as biologically linked to race, as in a typical article entitled "Never Blame the Genes," which warns,

If anyone thinks there is no link between race and crime, let him cast an eye on the following figures. . . . The usual excuse for black crime is poverty, but even when the other minorities are on the same or lower economic level, blacks still outkill, outrape, outassault and outburglarize other nonwhites three or four to one.[22]

Race is held responsible for every aspect of an individual's life and behavior, as well as those of groups and nations. A *New Order* article declares that nations "must possess a national spirit; and that spirit is inevitably determined by the blood of its people."[23]

Not surprisingly, the characteristics that identify whites are always found to be superior to the characteristics of nonwhites. Differences in intelligence or brain size, as well as the accomplishments of "Western civilization," are frequently referenced to construct the superiority of whites, and the beauty of white women is invoked to signal the superiority of white aesthetics. A *Thunderbolt* article proclaims, "The negro in our midst is an inferior being,"[24] while the superiority of whites is constructed through frequent reiterations, as in this *New Order* article:

> America and all civilized society are the exclusive products of White man's mind and muscle . . . the White race is the Master Race of the earth . . . the Master Builders, the Master Minds, and the Master Warriors of civilization. Without the White race, the world would still be a Stone Age swamp.[25]

CONSTRUCTING GENDER DIFFERENCE

Like racial difference, gender difference is posited as rooted in nature and biology. Throughout this discourse, great effort is taken constantly to reiterate, and thereby produce, the reality of gender difference. It is common for many of the periodicals to invent new words in order to distinguish between males and females and emphasize the importance of difference. For example, there are frequent references to Jewesses, Negresses, Mulatresses, WASPesses, Shebrews, etc.[26] Cynthia Fuchs Epstein argues that these terms serve as a form of symbolic segregation, reinforcing the illusion of deeper differences.[27]

Like racial difference, gender difference is imagined as not merely differences in physical characteristics, but differences in character and personality as well. For example, a *White Power* article explains that

> Our ancestors wisely realized that women were different from men not just biologically, but psychologically and emotionally as well. They recognized that the sexes had distinct but complementary roles to play in society . . . ordained by natural law.[28]

And like racial difference, sexual difference is believed to be a fact of nature and immutable. Articles in *Instauration* often attack those who do not recognize this "fact." For example, a typical article entitled "The One-Hemisphere Sex" wails,

> They never stop beating the nurture drum! A Purdue professor recently came up with the silly notion . . . that one reason for the superior mathematical ability of boys is they "are encouraged from an early age to do activities which develop spatial performance. . . ." So to

eliminate the different learning capabilities that separate the boys from the girls, Dr. Wheatley tells us the latter must learn to do more cogitating with their right hemispheres. That they don't do this and have never done this has nothing to do with genetics, of course. It has been the fault of their teachers—or a residue of Paleolithic prejudice—or male chauvinism.[29]

This article ridicules those who refuse to accept the "simple fact" that males and females are biologically different and thus unequal, and suggests that all other reasons for gender difference are simply excuses. As another *Instauration* article argues,

Boys are better at math than girls. . . . So far the best explanation of this true but "unacceptable" sexual difference in mental proficiency is that . . . "some of the genes contributing to intelligence are located on the sex chromosome."[30]

These articles suggest that while gender difference is genetic, it is "politically incorrect" to recognize this fact.

Both race and gender are constructed as genetic and/or God-given essences, and they are often interdependent. Gender and racial differences are linked throughout this discourse: the former are considered essential features distinguishing races from one another. A number of articles argue that the differences between the sexes are greatest in the white race.[31] Drawing upon the assumptions of early evolutionary theorists, differentiation is seen as the key to advancement. The more pronounced degree of differentiation between white men and women is offered as one factor separating whites from other races and signaling their supposed superiority. At the same time, males are posited as more differentiated than females, establishing white males as superior to white women and nonwhite men and women. As one author explains, "sexual dimorphism is greatest in the Caucasoids. We know further that women are less varied (smaller standard deviations) on most physical components, such as height, weight, and intelligence (relative brain size)."[32] This convenient matrix of differentiation perches white males firmly at the top.

While white supremacists cite the degree of gender difference between white men and women as one factor separating whites from other races and establishing white superiority, they also emphasize the differences between white and nonwhite females as a feature distinguishing the white race and signaling its superiority. The belief that white women represent the ideal of female beauty is widespread and considered commonsense knowledge in this discourse. An *Instauration* article credits "25,000 years of tough natural selection on the edge of glaciers" with producing "these beauteous products of a very special kind of evolution . . . these magnificent-looking women."[33] Further reflecting this sentiment, another article claims,

> the White woman stands at the apex of beauty. . . . But what about the Black woman? Alas, she is truly a pitiable creature. Whites have never found her attractive, and Blacks began to scorn her after they caught a glimpse of a White woman.[34]

An article entitled "White Is Beautiful" suggests that black women must be content with separate beauty pageants "because there is no way in which honest judges can compare the beauty of a White woman with that of an African woman."[35]

Attempting to establish the permanence and immutability of these differences, another article claims,

> Chinese archaeologists unearthed an ancient tomb containing a mummy of a female. They describe her as follows: "The shape of her body was extremely beautiful and she was tall. She had blond, long hair that flowed to her shoulders. On her comely face was a pair of big eyes. You could still count her long eyelashes. Beneath her high nose were her tiny, thin lips." The date of the remains indicated that gentlemen preferred blondes as early as 4480 B.C.[36]

DISEASE AND THE THREAT OF BOUNDARY CROSSING

The delineation of genetic differences frequently entails the description of diseases supposedly linked to race. For example, a *White Power* article entitled "Genetic Diseases Point Out Racial Differences" asserts that

> There are at least 13 separate diseases that strike only Jews of East European descent. . . . If the Jews are "only a religion"—as they love to claim—and not a racial group, how do the diseases know to strike only Jews and not Christians or atheists?[37]

While diseases are used to "point out racial differences," they also define nonwhite races as diseased and inferior. Another typical article entitled "Gene Scene" warns that

Blacks, Mediterraneans, Chinese, Filipinos and East Indians carry within their gene pools such biological shortcomings as thalassemia, sickle-cell anemia and a deficiency of the enzyme glucose-6-phosphate dehydrogenase.[38]

The diseases associated with nonwhites are often diseases tied to sexuality. For example, white supremacists link AIDS, gonorrhea, syphilis, and other sexually transmitted diseases to blacks, Jews, and other nonwhites. While the presence of these diseases define the nonwhite Other as inferior, it also establishes the Other as a threat to the health of whites. As an *NSV Report* article warns, in order to avoid AIDS, whites must avoid homosexuals and "the high risk racial groups which have a genetic susceptibility for AIDS which include Blacks and Hispanics."[39] An article in *The Thunderbolt* entitled "Haitians-Asians Bring Rare Diseases" notes that there is "a new strain of gonorrhea . . . brought to America by Southeast Asians and air force men who have consorted with Phillippino [*sic*] prostitutes."[40] An essay by The Order argues,

> No white person on earth would have AIDS if they did not engage in inter-racial sex. . . . The doctors and scientists who are searching for a cure are almost exclusively Jewish. This is not surprising in view of two facts: (a) All race-mixing has been promoted by the Jews through their total control of the media, politicians, government and judiciary. (b) Jews are the ultimate mongrel race.[41]

Through the depiction of the Other as diseased, white supremacists define interracial contact in general, and especially interracial sexuality, as a threat to the health of whites. An article in *Instauration* reveals that while "the progress of medical science and modern hygiene have practically banished cholera from the West" it is being brought back as the

> dirty water from aircraft following regular routes from Calcutta to Western Europe is unceremoniously dumped out during flight . . . unfriendly viruses and bacteria from Asia and Africa may also be riding the airways into Europe and North America.[42]

This discourse warns that contact between races, or the crossing of borders separating races (disease is often depicted as being carried across national borders by nonwhite immigrants), is a threat to white racial health.

Disease becomes a metaphor in this discourse, invoked again and again.[43]

Because racial differences are established as natural, white supremacists tie the separation of the races to racial health. Race-mixing, on the other hand, threatens racial difference and is equated with ill health, disease, and degeneration. White supremacists offer arguments indistinguishable from those put forth by eugenicists earlier this century. For example, a *White Power* article warns against the "sinister plot to make healthy people sick and clean people dirty. . . . The new America [must keep] its own people in a state of racial, cultural, and moral health."[44] Also echoing the assertions of many neoconservative scholars, contemporary society is defined as diseased for denying the inevitability of difference (read: inequality). As another article explains,

> the racial and political ills from which our Race suffers today are merely symptoms of a more profound *spiritual sickness*. . . . It is the goal of the New Order to attack the spiritual syphilis which is eating away at the soul of our Race . . . and to destroy the infection by massive doses of the proper antidote—the pure, undiluted medicine of the National Socialist world view. . . . *We live in a society which is completely out of harmony with the natural world* . . . the relationships between the races, between the sexes and between the generations— *everything* is out of sync with the natural order. . . . *Because of the unnatural, anti-natural society they live in and the lives they lead, White people have lost touch with the biological community to which they belong—their racial community.* . . . We will create a new society in which Nature and her laws are honored and venerated.[45]

The disruption of the binary oppositions through which identities are constructed as natural is depicted as "unnatural, anti-natural." A state of health is defined as the recognition of essential racial and gender identity and hierarchy and the maintenance of segregation.

THE NATURAL ORDER

If racial and gender differences are inherent and immutable, then it is fruitless to attempt to change them, and this is precisely what organized hate groups argue. For example, a *New Order* article explains that

> negroes are best suited for and succeed best in the roles of servants and entertainers. Remove the White liberal from his traditional posi-

tion, that is kissing the negro's posterior, and what happens to the negro? [He] clumsily shuffles off, scratching his wooley head, to search for shoebrush and mop. In the final debate, an ape will always be an ape.[46]

This article, like the quote introducing this chapter, recasts liberal egalitarians as perpetuating a cruel hoax and making unfair demands of African Americans. White supremacists, on the other hand, portray themselves as the only ones honest enough to recognize the natural limitations and capabilities of each race. The recognition of difference here is depicted as merely common sense, and this logic recasts white supremacists as benevolent truth seekers, just letting everyone "be themselves."

Equality necessarily entails the denial of difference throughout the various periodicals and is referred to as a hoax, myth, or lie. The *National Vanguard* cautions that equality is "Man's Most Dangerous Myth" because it denies "the essence of the inner nature."[47] An *Instauration* article entitled "The Hoax of All the Centuries" warns that "the real hoax is the equalitarian hoax, the hoax of hoaxes, the universal lie that there are no differences in racial intelligence." In order to counter this hoax, racial differences are documented further: "the average white six-year-old has a mental age of six; the average black six-year-old a mental age of five. At age 12 the average white has a mental age of 12; the average black a mental age of 10."[48]

If differences are rooted in nature or preordained by God, it is a waste of time to attempt to change them. As an *NS Mobilizer* article explains,

> human evolution and social progress depend on the natural ascendance of the strong, the creative, the energetic . . . and the *natural submission* of the weak, the stupid, and the lazy; and that the world's wealth and resources must not be squandered on the very elements whom *nature* has rejected.[49]

The maintenance of the boundaries sustaining the white/black and male/female dichotomies is required, and threats to the maintenance of those boundaries are threats to the construction of racial and gender identities themselves. Disease becomes one metaphor in this discourse for the threat of boundary transgressions.

The production of racial and gender difference is central to the project of white supremacy. Binary oppositions serve to preserve white privilege and racial hierarchy. Epstein argues that "dichotomous systems of thought

serve the existing power structures and organization of society by reinforcing the notion of the 'we' and the 'not-we,' the deserving and the undeserv-
ing."[50] Every white supremacist periodical I have seen spends a great deal
of space and effort documenting and reiterating dichotomous racial differences and often gender differences as well. Furthermore, the construction
of race and gender is clearly intertwined and occurs within the difference/
equality framework. Any attempts to increase equality are therefore recast
as threats to difference. In order to secure difference and domination, then,
maintenance of the boundaries is *essential*, and we shall explore this process
in the following chapters.

NOTES

1. *White Power* March 1973, 3–6.
2. Scott 1988a, 39.
3. *Instauration* February 1980, 13.
4. *Instauration* January 1980, 15.
5. *The Thunderbolt* no. 301, 6.
6. *The New Order* March 1990, 2.
7. *White Power* March 1973, 6.
8. *Instauration* January 1980, 21.
9. *The Thunderbolt* January 1974, 10.
10. Ridgeway 1990.
11. Butler 1993a, 2.
12. Butler 1991, 24.
13. *Instauration* October 1976, 10.
14. *Instauration* September 1979, 17.
15. Seidman 1991, 135.
16. *The Thunderbolt* August 1979, 8.
17. *Instauration* March 1980, 16.
18. *National Vanguard* special issue, 3.
19. *NSV Report* October/December 1991, 3.
20. *The Thunderbolt* 30 May 1975, 8.
21. *NSV Report* October/December 1987, 1.
22. *Instauration* September 1979, 19.
23. *The New Order* March 1979, 1.
24. *The Thunderbolt* no. 277(May 1982), 3.

25. *The New Order* no. 23(March 1979), 8.
26. *Instauration* December 1979, 13; *Instauration* February 1981; *The New Order* March 1979, 2.
27. Epstein 1988.
28. *White Power* no. 105, 4.
29. *Instauration* September 1979, 19.
30. *Instauration* April 1981, 18.
31. *Instauration* January 1980, 14–15.
32. *Instauration* March 1981, 7.
33. *Instauration* May 1981, 36.
34. *National Vanguard* May 1979, 11.
35. *The Thunderbolt* September 1981, 10.
36. *Instauration* May 1981, 23.
37. *White Power* no. 91(April 1979), 5.
38. *Instauration* February 1981, 20.
39. *NSV Report* October/December 1987, 8.
40. *The Thunderbolt* May 1982, 4.
41. Coates 1987, 203.
42. *Instauration* September 1979, 18.
43. Sontag 1978.
44. *White Power* July 1973, 3.
45. *White Power* no. 104, 1.
46. *The New Order* September 1979, 14.
47. *National Vanguard* no. 68, 3.
48. *Instauration* April 1981, 13.
49. *NS Mobilizer* July/August 1974, 11.
50. Epstein 1988, 233.

IT ALL COMES DOWN TO SEXUALITY

Interracial Sexuality and the
Threat to Difference

What's wrong with interracial sex? Well, interracial sex is immoral and unscientific. Also, interracial sex has destroyed many civilizations. What dark races have ever contributed anything to civilization comparable to the light bulb, the airplane or the automobile? A famous U.S. Senator once stated that all our armies, cities and machines could be destroyed—and we could rebuild. But he went on to say that the White Christian Race could never be restored if it were destroyed through racial mongrelization.[1]

White supremacist discourse is obsessed with interracial sexuality. This point cannot be overemphasized. Newsletters devote huge amounts of space to the issue. Perusing a few publications yields a plethora of titles decrying the phenomenon: "More Mixed Breeds Born,"[2] "God Commanded Racial Segregation; Holy Bible Condemns Mixed Marriage," "Brainwashed Into Interracial Marriage," "Mixed Babies are Colored,"[3] "Mixed Marriage Mongrelizing Russia,"[4] and "Interracial Marriages On Increase."[5] These articles frequently accompany photographs of interracial couples or mixed-race children (see figure 3).[6]

These articles usually emphasize the horrific consequences for those engaging in interracial sexuality. "Mongrels Live Miserable Lives" according to a column in *The Thunderbolt*, which presents what is introduced as a letter from a mixed-race woman who warns, "I know the unhappiness of our kind. It is a sin to bring people into the world who are burdened with the consequence of race mixture. This gives rise to anguish and it is the work of the devil."[7] Another article warns that the "Innocent Suffer From Mixed Couples," describing the plight of white women led to lives of crime because of their involvement with black men.[8]

THE THREAT TO RACIAL DIFFERENCE

Within the difference versus equality framework, threats to white hegemony are cast as threats to differentiation. White supremacist groups view the civil rights movement, gay and lesbian rights movement, and feminism as efforts to erase human differences and make all people the same. Interracial sexuality emerges as the most evocative symbol of this threat.

While white supremacist discourse enshrines differentiation as the key to advancement and the natural path of evolution, it paints interracial sexuality as threatening differentiation and progress. Within this discursive framework, supremacists argue that their fight against interracial sexuality is a struggle to "preserve diversity" and compare preserving human diversity with efforts to preserve the diversity of species. One article from a white supremacist tract complains that there is no protest against interracial marriage, "yet they delay a dam project to save the snail darter."[9] Another article compares racial preservation to historical preservation efforts:

> The fact that the world is being overrun with houses doesn't stop us from protecting unusual ones. The *only* field in which it is not respectable to advocate the preservation of diversity is when it has to do with human appearance. Here we're all supposed to become a drab, look-alike brown.[10]

Interracial sexuality, it is suggested, will erase differences and make everyone the same: brown. Cannibalizing liberal notions of the value of diversity, white supremacists argue that separation of the races is necessary in order to preserve human diversity. White supremacists depict *themselves* as the true guardians of racial diversity who must struggle against interracial sexuality and other threats to racial differentiation. This manipulation certainly highlights the problem with liberal conceptions of diversity that ground themselves in essentialist racial classifications.

Other white supremacist articles argue that interracial sexual relationships will not only make everyone look the same, but will actually reverse
evolutionary processes that have created different races:

> Interracism would reverse the process of divergent evolution by fusing
> the races back together in a genetic recoalescence in which the traits,
> qualities, and aesthetic ideal of Northern man would be destroyed. . . .
> These Northerners who practice . . . sexual interracism, are following
> the path to racial oblivion.[11]

Or, put even more succinctly, they "VIOLATE THE LAW OF GOD AND
NATURE BY SEXUALLY UNITING WITH THE INFERIOR RACES!"[12]

Gender differences are similarly constructed in essentialist, binary terms.
Like traditional definitions of sex and gender, white supremacist discourse
"posits two fixed, static, and mutually exclusive role containers with no inter-
penetration. Further, bipolar mutual exclusivity of sex roles reinforces oppositional assumptions about masculinity and femininity."[13] Any reduction of
differences between men and women is taken as a sign of the degeneration
of our society. For example, an article entitled "Women Reduced to Fighting" asserts that "women who resort to the martial arts type of hand-to-hand
fighting are safest from attackers. . . . Civilization is going down fast when
our womenfolk are reduced to such a level."[14] An *Instauration* article makes
a similar argument, displaying a poster for a gladiator show that advertises
"The Toughest Guy in South Florida Competition Plus 'Toughest Woman
Competition.' " The article retorts "Gladiator contests have often been considered a sign of the Roman Empire's decline. But as far as we know, even
the Romans didn't have women gladiators."[15] These articles and others reify
masculinity and femininity as oppositional and suggest that the performance
of masculine activities by females is a sign of our society's decline.

FROM INTEGRATION TO INTERCOURSE

Extending the previous argument, white supremacists construe any attempt to increase racial or gender equality as a direct threat to the white
race: not only to white power and hegemony, but to the very existence of
the white race. White supremacist publications are flooded with articles that
warn against " 'Civil Rights,' 'Integration,' 'busing'—no matter what you call

it, the reality is the same: race-mixing."[16] Desegregation becomes an attempt to increase interracial sexuality, to produce sameness. As an article in *The Thunderbolt* explains,

> the main reason our forefathers opposed socializing with blacks was because they knew from history that it led to the bedroom and interracial breeding. The only reason our people are not half-breed mongrels today is because our ancestors preached and practiced SEGREGATION OF THE RACES.[17]

Integration and interracial sexuality become closely linked throughout white supremacist publications.

School desegregation is another popular focus of articles dealing with integration and always including or implying concerns about sexual intimacy. A typical article in *The Thunderbolt* asserts that "when schools are integrated—by busing or other means—black teenagers soon start dating whites. . . . Racial busing leads to interracial sex and mongrel babies."[18] A typical article in *The New Order* entitled "The Real Face of Integration" warns that "the result of unnaturally mingling White children with the offspring of lesser races" will lead to the mongrelization of the race.[19] Photographs often appear next to these articles, showing white and black children side-by-side, embracing, as in figure 4.[20] The accompanying article, entitled "Fruits of Mythical Racial Equality," explains, "this is how it begins. Interracial relationships begin in school and result in the mongrelization of the White Race."[21]

Interracial sexuality is not merely attacked as an indirect result, or side effect, of integration. *The Thunderbolt* asserts that when the Supreme Court

> outlaw[ed] racial segregation in the schools, it was for the evil purpose of promoting social contact between innocent little White children and the inferior black race that would bring about interracial marriage and the mongrelization of the White Race[22]

and "mongrelization of the White Race [was] the planned end result!"[23] For white supremacists, the goal and sole purpose of desegregation efforts are the promotion of interracial sexuality and miscegenation.

Articles focusing on school integration manipulate parental concern and depict white children at risk. "Whites Tormented in Mixed Schools," "Mother Refuses to Send Daughter, 8, to School," and other similar articles describe rapes and torturings of white children by black classmates.[24] These articles especially beseech parents to protect their daughters. Articles abound with titles like "Integration Leads White Girls into Trouble."[25] An inflammatory recruitment flyer for the National Socialist White People's Party warns that

> the genocide isn't so slow anymore. Now they want to offer up our precious sons and daughters—our FUTURE!—to the slobbering baboons waiting for them in what these rotten federal creeps call schools nowadays. . . . Well, what are you going to do about it, Whitey? Are you just going to sit there and let your kids go down the drain . . . your girls . . . felt up, seduced or even raped by gibbering he-niggers?[26]

Integrated housing is also attacked. A *White Power* article explains,

> Now that the busses are rolling on their genocidal journey of bringing White and Negro children forcibly together in the schools, our Jew-dominated government is moving relentlessly on to the next step: forced mixing of the races in housing . . . to carry out the lunatic program of interbreeding.[27]

An *Instauration* article warns, "It is not black power that we need to fear. We should fear black coexistence in the same living space . . . once our race is gone because of integration with blacks, we are done."[28]

A *Thunderbolt* article asserts in its title that " 'Destroy Racism' Means Mongrelize Whites."

> The time has come for White Americans everywhere to understand what this monstrous fight against "Racism" actually is. It is a diabolical movement to implant such a deep seated guilt complex within our people that we willingly will join the march behind the Judas goat into the abyss of racial suicide!![29]

This article recasts "The fight to abolish 'Racism' " as nothing more than "a struggle to obliterate the White Race from the face of this earth!"

The threat of interracial sexuality is deployed everywhere. While there has been a widespread backlash against affirmative action depicting it as a form of "reverse racism," white supremacists assert that affirmative action was developed as part of a purposeful plan to destroy the white race. According to this logic, affirmative action and egalitarian movements in general are simply a disguise for attacking whites. An *NSV Report* contends that affirmative action is not really about giving jobs to disadvantaged minorities but part of the bigger conspiracy:

> the Jews are busy with genocide in a very subtle manner. It is done through government policy. A White man goes to a government employment office. He is on the bottom of the totem pole by Federal law. All non-Whites get first crack at all the jobs. The government does not want White men to have the money to raise a White family. It is called keeping the White birth rate as low as possible. The government would rather keep a White woman employed rather than a White man because this keeps the White woman out of the home and on the job.[30]

Elsewhere, affirmative action programs are described as plans to bring black men and white women together in the workplace to encourage sexual activity between them. A *National Vanguard* article warns, "integration is just a code word for racemixing. Civil rights for Black men do not really mean equal employment opportunities; they mean equal enjoyment opportunities with White women."[31] Other articles describe rapes of white women by black men in the workplace. A *Thunderbolt* article presents the case of white nurses working in hospitals with "high quotas of negroes." After describing the rape of one woman, the article concludes that "because of the aggressive hostility on the part of blacks, life has been made miserable for the White girls working in hospitals."[32] Figure 5 further demonstrates this, suggesting that affirmative action for white women is nothing more than a ploy to increase interracial sexuality between white women and black men.[33]

Other articles link affirmative action to increased integrated housing, claiming,

> People marry those they go to school with, grow up with, socialize with and who they live close to [and more blacks] are moving to the White suburbs . . . under the gun of so-called "Affirmative action hiring quotas." As they make more money they can afford to buy into White neighborhoods.[34]

While clearly a threat to white economic privilege, this threat is rearticulated primarily as the spectre of interracial sexuality.

According to white supremacist discourse, people are naturally attracted

Figures 1a and 1b:
"The White Patriot
Party strives to make
activism compatible
with family life.
Many members are
married couples."
(*The Spotlight,*
20 January 1986, 16)

The photos reproduced
here give a sense of
how white supremacist
literature treats racial
topics visually. In most
cases original prints were
not available; their
diminished photographic
quality results from
secondary printing from
archival copies of the
publications.

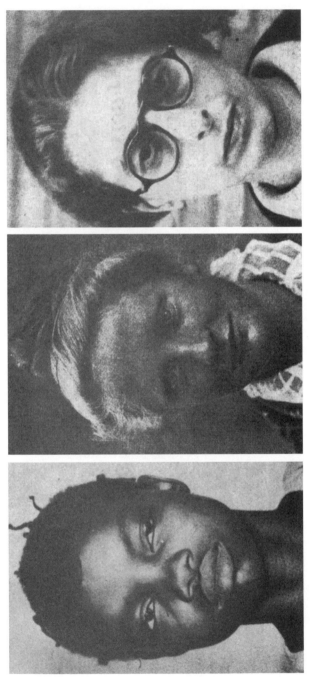

Figure 2: "*Equality—Man's Most Dangerous Myth.* ONLY THE FOOL or the mischief-maker can claim that the same soul dwells in the breast of the Negro, the White, and the Jew." (*National Vanguard*, special issue, 3)

Figure 3: "THE ME-CENTERED ethic which has been promoted with great success in the West since the Second World War demands no responsibility from the individual to anything beyond himself: not to his race, not to family or tribal traditions, not to Life. The only proper goal for the individual is happiness. If he or she believes the road to personal happiness is to bed down with a non-White and produce pickaninnies, why that's no one else's business, according to those governed by this ethic." (*National Vanguard*, August 1982, 15)

Figure 4: *"Fruits of Mythical Racial Equality:* This is how it begins. Interracial relationships begin in school and result in the mongrelization of the White race." (*The Thunderbolt*, September 1981, 3)

Figure 5: ERA leads to interracial sexuality. (*The Thunderbolt*, February 1980, 12)

Figure 6: *"Endangered Species:* It's worth more than a thousand words to know that there's still something worth living and dying for despite the seemingly hopeless shape of our civilization. Instead of the present social mess of deviant sex, rampant divorce and abortions, this little girl serves as a call to all decent White people to live for a purpose once again." (*White Power*, December 1980, 9)

Figure 7: "Will there be room in a darkening America for these children?" (*National Vanguard*, May 1978, 1)

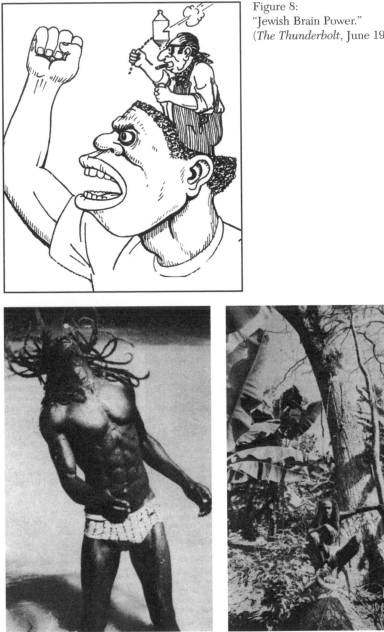

Figure 8:
"Jewish Brain Power."
(*The Thunderbolt*, June 1975, 8)

Figures 9a and 9b: "RASTAFARIANS consciously cultivate an image of Black
Tarzans in order to attract White women." (*National Vanguard*, January 1983, 21)

Figure 10: "ONLY THE STORMTROOPER CAN STOP THIS: There's no easy way out of this mess. So stand with us—or stand out of our way!" (*White Power*, September 1973, 6)

Figure 11: "ENDANGERED SPECIES? Healthy, beautiful children such as these are our Race's most precious resource. Yet . . . so many White couples of childbearing age are choosing to have only one or two off-spring—or none at all." (*White Power,* no. 101, 1)

Figure 12: "MOTHER AND CHILD—What White person who has healthy instincts and spiritual attitudes could fail to be moved by this photograph? Yet if this woman doesn't have three or more children during her lifetime she is helping to speed her Race along the road to extinction." (*White Power,* no. 101, 3)

to their own kind and naturally repelled by those of other races, but integration breaks down that natural revulsion. An *Instauration* article expounds,

when different races are forced into a constant condition of unnaturally close proximity, the degree of sensitivity and discrimination in the selection of sexual partners tends to decrease markedly as the formerly strong sense of sexual revulsion is eroded.[35]

The white guilt complex and white fears of being labeled "racist" are presented as another tool to break down this "natural" sense of "revulsion." Numerous articles throughout the periodicals present guilt as a primary tool used to increase interracial sexuality. For example, the goal of multicultural curricula is, of course, to increase interracial sexuality by instilling "self-hate and a guilt complex in young Whites so they will tolerate Non-White domination and interracial marriage."[36] An *Instauration* article suggests that even though whites find blacks naturally "revulsive," if a woman

rejects the sexual advances of non-Northern Europeans, she may wonder about her motives and be plagued by self-recriminations on the suspicion that her rejection of the non-Northern European was motivated by "prejudice." In her attempt to repent and prove that she is not a racist, which she has been taught to believe is the greatest of all immoralities, she overcompensates and engages in profligate, self-sacrificing interracism . . . to avoid feelings of guilt.[37]

Here, the label "racist" is a tool to intimidate whites into inactivity. *The Turner Diaries*, a futuristic novel considered the blueprint for the Oklahoma City bombing, presents a picture of society where white women and young girls are constantly raped and attacked by black men, and white men never protest out of fear that it would be racist. As the narrator explains, "Even when gangs of Blacks took their children away or raped their women before their eyes, they offered no significant resistance . . . many of them seem to be convinced that any effort at self-defense would be 'racist.' "[38]

The novel depicts the case of Elsa, a young white girl harassed and attacked by the black boys in her integrated school:

When a Black assistant principal cornered her in his office one day and tried to put his hand inside her dress . . . Elsa came home from school in tears and begged her parents to send her to another school. Her mother's response was to scream at her, slap her face, and call her a "racist." If the Black boys were bothering her, it was her fault, not theirs.[39]

Later in the novel, once the race revolution is under way and the military and police are out in full force, Turner describes the following scene:

> two grinning Black soldiers forced their way through the throng in front of the tent and went inside, dragging a terrified, sobbing White girl about 14 years old between them. The raping queue moved forward another space. I ran over to a White officer [and] began angrily protesting what was happening, but [he] turned shamefacedly away from me and hurried off in the opposite direction. Two White soldiers nearby cast their eyes downward and disappeared between two tents. No one wanted to be suspected of "racism."[40]

Rather than a movement for social justice and equality, according to white supremacists the fight against racism is a mere cover-up for the outright attack against the white race, via its women and girls, with the goal of increasing interracial sexuality and mongrelizing the white race out of existence. Indeed, the NAACP is defined in this discourse as nothing more than an "organization to advertise the Negro to Whites . . . to carry out 'the great ideal of Judaism' on race-mixing."[41] Any attempt to question the hierarchy of the white/black dichotomy is cast as a threat to the dichotomy itself, threatening to eliminate whiteness, which acquires its existence through that very dichotomy.

In chapter three, we saw that, historically, economic and political freedom for blacks was opposed on the grounds that it would increase interracial sexuality. Just as "Southern white determination to maintain the Jim Crow system was symbolized by the firmly held belief that the sexual and racial purity of white womanhood had to be protected,"[42] the contemporary white supremacist response to movements for racial equality continues to hold forth this image. The threat of interracial sexuality is again relied upon to justify segregation and attack economic and political equality, which are depicted as nothing more than attacks against whites. Within this system of logic, white supremacists can contend that they are only trying to defend themselves and protect their racial brethren.

THE FEMINIST THREAT

The women's movement is among the most popular targets of white supremacists. Feminism is represented as a threat to gender difference because it questions gender stratification and inequality. Consequently, feminists are constantly accused of wanting to make males and females the same. As *The Turner Diaries* describes it,

> "Women's lib" was a form of mass psychosis. . . . Women affected by it denied their femininity and insisted that they were "people," not "women." This aberration was promoted and encouraged by the system as a means of dividing our race against itself.[43]

One of the scenarios described in this utopian novel presents the result of feminism carried to what is described as its logical end:

> the Supreme Court ruled that all laws making rape a crime are unconstitutional, because they presume a legal difference between the sexes. Rape, the judges ruled, can only be prosecuted under the statutes covering non-sexual assaults. . . . In other words, rape has been reduced to the status of a punch in the nose. . . . The women's-lib groups have greeted this development with dismay. It isn't exactly what they had in mind when they began agitating for "equality" two decades ago. . . . Nowadays gangs of Black thugs hang around parking lots and school playgrounds and roam the corridors of office buildings and apartment complexes, looking for any attractive, unescorted White girl and knowing that punishment, either from the disarmed citizenry or the handcuffed police, is extremely unlikely. Gang rapes in school classrooms have become an especially popular new sport.[44]

"Women's lib" here ironically leads to violence against women because it erases gender difference. Once again any questioning of difference is construed as an argument for sameness. Feminism is also feared as a threat to racial difference, as is evident in the preceding examples. Feminism is widely referred to as a tool for dividing the white race, increasing interracial sexuality, and erasing racial difference.

A regular column in *Instauration*, entitled "The Majority Under Siege," lists incidences that supposedly depict whites under attack. In one column I discovered the following: "In Princeton University, Sally Franks, '80, tried to force the all-male eating clubs to accept her as a member."[45] The inclusion of this incident in this particular column further demonstrates the interconnections among gender and racial differences within this discourse. A threat to gender difference is a threat to racial difference. Any attack on what has been constructed as a natural, essential difference is construed as an attack on all forms of human difference, on the very possibility of difference.

WHERE HAVE ALL THE REAL MEN GONE?

The threat of interracial sexuality is emphasized in elaborations of declining white masculinity in which white males are depicted as effeminate. This effeminacy is targeted as a cause of interracial sexuality. As one article explains,

> Northern European males have traditionally tended throughout history to be dominant by nature, but . . . they are becoming submissive and passive. This phenomenon is especially obvious in the declining strength of their opposition to the interracial sexual transgressions of non-Northern European males with Northern European females. [Northern European men] repress the natural inborn tendencies of exclusivity which played an important role in preserving the biological integrity of their race during its evolution. Many carry their altruism to the point of even seeming to approve of, and to encourage, the sexual trespasses of non-Northern European males upon Northern European females whom their more vigorous and race-conscious ancestors would have defended from such defilements with their very lives.[46]

The author laments the destruction of what he sees as the natural roles of men and women, attacking contemporary white men, no longer "real men" willing to prove their masculinity by protecting white women. The breakdown of these natural roles threatens to increase interracial sexuality and lead to the subsequent breakdown of the natural racial order. According to white supremacist discourse, protecting women was traditionally a primary component in the definition of masculinity, and today's men are therefore no longer behaving like men. White men are blamed for allowing "their" women to fall into the arms of black men. This decline in white masculinity is targeted as a primary reason for the increase in interracial sexuality. Changing gender relations are held responsible for the destruction of white racial identity.

In an article entitled "Sexuality in a Sick Society," subtitled "The Changing Relationship between Men and Women is Leading to Ominous Racial

Consequences for the West," we are told that feminism and the sexual revolution have led to the

> demasculinization of the Western male, [and] together with the reaction of the Western female to this, [it] is a cause for grave concern . . . [men] are constrained from expressing their maleness in any of the ways which were natural in the past. One of the most important of those ways was protecting a mate. . . . All the brave, new talk about marriage today being a partnership of equals does not change the basic, biological natures of men and women. Those natures have fitted them for *complimentary* roles, not for the *same* role . . . [but now the man is no longer] the master in his house. One way in which Western women have responded to the perceived demasculinization of their men has been to turn toward non-White males, who are perceived as more masculine . . . [a woman will] run through a long succession of Black lovers in her fruitless, instinctual search for a man who would not only love her but also master her.[47]

The sexual revolution is blamed for the demasculinization of white men, who can no longer stand up and protect their property, white females. Attempts to try to change what is constructed as the biological nature of men and women have transformed white males into "whimps" unable to satisfy white women's need to be controlled and mastered, forcing white women to turn to black males. A threat to the "natural" gender order is synonymous with a threat to the "natural" racial order. This *National Vanguard* article succinctly summarizes the situation, highlighting the interlocking nature of race and gender identity: "it is a grim reminder to us of the inextricable interdependence of the sexual and racial issues: Unless a healthy relationship between the sexes is reestablished in the West, the White race certainly will not survive."[48]

In white supremacist discourse, a threat to the racial dichotomy and hierarchy is a threat to what is constructed as the natural racial order. Similarly, a threat to the gender dichotomy and hierarchy is a threat to what is constructed as the natural gender order. They are threats to the binary oppositions of male/female and white/nonwhite and are represented as threats to *difference* itself. Any threat to gender difference is therefore also a threat to racial difference, and any threat to racial difference is constructed as a threat to gender difference. Like a row of dominoes, it is assumed that if one is knocked over, the others will surely follow.

NOTES

1. *The Thunderbolt* April 1975, 10.
2. *The Thunderbolt* January 1979, 8.
3. *The Thunderbolt* May 1981, 7.
4. *The Thunderbolt* July 1981, 12.
5. *The Thunderbolt* August 1981, 4.
6. *National Vanguard* August 1982, 15.
7. *The Thunderbolt* August 1979, 9.
8. *The Thunderbolt* May 1981, 5.
9. *Instauration* January 1980, 14.
10. *Instauration* January 1980, 14.
11. *Instauration* June 1980, 6.
12. *The Thunderbolt* May 1981, 5.
13. Kimmel 1987, 123.
14. *The Thunderbolt* May 1982, 3.
15. *Instauration* March 1981, 30.
16. *White Power* March 1972, 3.
17. *The Thunderbolt* August 1980, 3.
18. *The Thunderbolt* 25 April 1975, 10.
19. *The New Order* September 1979, 7.
20. *The Thunderbolt* September 1981, 3.
21. *The Thunderbolt* September 1981, 3.
22. *The Thunderbolt* August 1981, 8.
23. *The Thunderbolt* August 1979, 1.
24. *The Thunderbolt* January 1979, 8.
25. *The Thunderbolt* January 1979, 12.
26. NSWPP flyer entitled "Boating Not Busing!"
27. *White Power* March 1972, 3.
28. *Instauration* April 1980, 13–14.
29. *The Thunderbolt* 30 May 1975, 3.
30. *NSV Report* January/March 1989, 1.
31. *National Vanguard* May 1979, 11.
32. *The Thunderbolt* 30 May 1975, 8.
33. *The Thunderbolt* February 1980, 12.
34. *The Thunderbolt* August 1980, 3.
35. *Instauration* June 1980, 7.
36. *The Thunderbolt* March 1982, 3.

37. *Instauration* June 1980, 7.
38. Macdonald 1978, 152.
39. Macdonald 1978, 83.
40. Macdonald 1978, 187.
41. *White Power* March 1972, 3.
42. Davis 1991, 78.
43. Macdonald 1978, 45.
44. Macdonald 1978, 57–58.
45. *Instauration* September 1980, 25.
46. *Instauration* June 1980, 8.
47. *National Vanguard* January 1983, 17.
48. *National Vanguard* January 1983, 21–22.

7

BOUNDARY TRANSGRESSIONS

"The Death of the White Race." This provocative heading on a flyer distributed by Aryan Nations is meant to capture viewers' attention and entice them to read on.[1] Beneath the prominent heading is a photograph of a white woman with her arms wrapped around the neck of a black man with the caption "The Ultimate Abomination." Throughout white supremacist discourse, interracial sexual relationships are defined as the greatest threat, the worst thing imaginable. At the root of white supremacist anxiety and fear over various other issues lies an obsession with interracial sexuality, and interracial sexuality is the convenient threat deployed to guard against intrusions upon white male political and economic dominance.

There has been a great deal of white supremacist violence aimed at interracial couples and mixed-race families.[2] On September 8, 1992, in Spokane, Washington, "a man walked into the downtown Greyhound bus station, pulled a .38 caliber handgun from his belt and fired five shots without warning" at a young couple. They were shot and wounded because the man was black and the woman was white. As the assailant explained, "I just knew they should die because of what they had done. I think he put his arm around her or something."[3]

Interracial sexuality becomes a metaphor for all boundary transgressions and menaces binary racial and gender identities. Anxiety over border maintenance suffuses contemporary white supremacist discourse, which is preoccupied with the bodily integrity of individuals, races, and nations. The threat of disease is but one manifestation of this obsession. These various borders overlap and are overdetermined with meaning, so that the regulation of individual bodies symbolizes the protection of racial and geographical borders and vice versa. The same language of boundary maintenance is used to discuss the penetration of individual and community bodily boundaries. Immigration provides a perfect example of this.

While blacks and Jews are the vilest enemies preoccupying racist organizations, other racial groups are discussed, especially in terms of immigration policy. Nonwhite immigration is often posited as a threat to white America in articles such as "Colored Immigration Our No. 1 Problem,"[4] "Alien Hordes Become Citizens,"[5] and "Illegal Aliens Threaten America!"[6] While blacks and Jews are most often the focus of hatred in white supremacist publications, all nonwhites are defined as a threat:

> America is being invaded by a deluge of legal and illegal non-White intruders: swarms of Mexican, Puerto Rican, Negro, Oriental and Jewish scum who are thronging across our wide-open borders . . . catastrophe will devastate our United States and exterminate our Aryan Race unless the unarmed invasion of the inferior and unassimilable is not only stopped, but totally reversed in a violent and massive racial purge.[7]

Immigration is described in the same terms as those used for the threats of disease and interracial sexuality: an invasion or penetration of the white body by the nonwhite Other. Terms like "penetration," "infestation," "pollution," and "invasion" are used to describe all of these phenomena. Disease and immigration describe, on a larger scale, the phenomenon of interracial sexuality: all are posited as a threat to a racially pure white body and are described as leading to the mongrelization and genocide of the white race. The images of these three overlap; immigrants are often described as "disease-ridden,"[8] and, as a *New Order* article asserts, more and more "foreign students are enrolled in U.S. colleges . . . the 'students' will be dating and marrying the more intelligent American White girls."[9] Nonwhite immigration, we see, becomes the threat of interracial sexuality. Individual (specifically female), racial, and national boundaries are confounded: a threat to one is a threat to all.

Just as the body of America is considered threatened with pollution from nonwhite immigrants penetrating its borders, interracial sexuality is defined as the pollution of the white female body by a nonwhite male. It is always the white woman whose bodily boundaries are at risk of being penetrated. In white supremacist discourse, it is the white female body that must be protected and regulated in the name of the race. Within the regulation of heterosexual relations, it is the relationship between white women and black men that is a threat; only the white woman's bodily integrity and coherence are constructed as vulnerable to invasion. Given that the female body represents the racial community, this penetration of the female body symbolizes the pollution of the white race. Expanding upon the work of anthropologist Mary Douglas, Judith Butler asserts that the concept of pollution

> "expresses a desire to keep the body (physical and social) intact," suggesting that the naturalized notion of "the" body is itself a consequence of taboos that render that body discrete by virtue of its stable boundaries.[10]

Like the threats of disease and immigration, the metaphor of pollution is frequently invoked to represent the danger of border crossings. For example, a *Thunderbolt* article defines pollution as

> the placement of unacceptable elements into an organization, group or body of agreeable elements. It will always lead to destruction of one or all elements. . . . Pollution of blood: Blood is responsible for our inheritance. It can cause us to be idiot or genius, sick or healthy, white or black. We have inferior or superior blood. Superior specimen, crossbreeding with inferior specimen, must become inferior in the end.[11]

Interracial sexuality is depicted as polluting whiteness.

Taboos against interracial sexuality serve to construct and exaggerate the differences between white and black. The construction and maintenance of the white/black binary opposition produces racialized bodies, and the regulation of interracial sexuality is necessary to maintain the dichotomy. Culturally intelligible racialized and gendered bodies are produced through the maintenance of boundaries, and interracial sexuality represents the ultimate threat to these dichotomies. Symbolizing the transgression of racial boundaries, interracial sexuality threatens the assumption of stable, pure, racial identities, the construction of which is the central project of white supremacist discourse.

Interracial sexual relationships are a threat to the possibility of a white identity and are therefore defined as not simply acts between individuals but between races. As a *National Alliance Bulletin* article explains,

> *Any contact between a White person and a member of any other race is, both actually and symbolically, a contact between the two races as*

a whole, and not just a contact between individuals. Thus, a White person who has sexual relations with a non-White defiles not only himself but also the White race, and he must, therefore, be held answerable to the White racial community as a whole for his crime.[12]

The transgressive acts of an individual threaten the entire community; indeed, they threaten the very possibility of a white identity.

White supremacist discourse argues that if a white woman has intercourse once with a black male, her body is forever polluted. A *Thunderbolt* article entitled "Sexual Contact With Negro Can Result In Black Baby By White Parents" warns that a white woman who is impregnated by a black man is infected with black blood, from the baby through the umbilical cord, which then enters her entire body. Extending this argument even further, the article warns that

> even . . . without impregnation, sexual intercourse with a black male leads to an infusion of the black sperm into the system of the White female which affects her body chemistry toward negroidal traits . . . a White woman who engaged in sex with negroes should be considered no longer to be a part of the White Race . . . negroidal influence can show up in future births . . . she has in a chemical way become part of the black race even though she still has the appearance of a White person.[13]

Thus, interracial sexuality, whether it results in a child or not, is defined as the pollution of the white race because it represents the transgression of racial boundaries and the penetration and pollution of the white community by the black racial Other.

It is the white female and the black male, then, who are seen as polluting persons in white supremacist discourse. According to Butler, Mary Douglas explains that

> "A polluting person is always in the wrong. He has developed some wrong condition or simply crossed over some line which should not have been crossed and this displacement unleashes danger for someone." . . . If the body is synecdochal for the social system *per se* or a site in which open systems converge, then any kind of unregulated permeability constitutes a site of pollution and endangerment.[14]

It is only the black male and white female bodies that are the target of regulations governing interracial sexual relations.

TARGET: WHITE WOMEN AND BLACK MEN

While interracial sexuality between all whites and all nonwhites is taboo in this discourse, the plethora of images and articles about interracial sexuality focuses almost exclusively on white women and black men. Robert J. C. Young describes this as a central ambivalence in colonial discourse, characterized by both desire and aversion.[15] He elaborates on this in his analysis of nineteenth-century racist discourse, and we find this same ambivalence in contemporary white supremacist discourse. While relationships between white women and black men are condemned, and described as repulsive, relationships between white men and black women were common and remain beyond condemnation. We find no references to these relationships in white supremacist publications—but not because they do not occur. Yet, even the relationships between white women and black men serve and reveal white male desire. White men continue to produce and consume detailed images and descriptions of these affairs. The overwhelming number of these images throughout white supremacist discourse, while endlessly attacked, betrays some element of desire on the part of those who obsessively reproduce and read these images.

The image of a white woman with a black man is relied upon throughout the discourse and serves as a powerful metaphor for the danger of interracial sexuality. This image has a long, entrenched history. As we witnessed in chapter three, the image of the lustful, dangerous black male is firmly rooted in, and reiterated throughout, American history. The edited collection *Reading Rodney King/Reading Urban Uprising* highlights the power this image still retains and its entrenchment in American thought. Editor Robert Gooding-Williams points out that in the trial of the police officers accused of beating King, the defense attorneys drew upon "a mode of perception that insists always and everywhere on seeing black bodies as dangerous bodies."[16] Linking the beating of King with a tradition rooted in slavery, Ruth Wilson Gilmore's essay suggests to Gooding-Williams that "the beating of Rodney King was an act of 'civilized terror' belonging to a firmly established American tradition of white-on-black violence, the most prominent examples of which are racial lynchings."[17]

This narrative, which defines black males as animalistic and savage, is central to white American identity, and, as Houston A. Baker reminds us, "this scene plays itself out . . . with infinite variation in American history."[18]

As the Rodney King beating and trial confirm, this racialized–gendered narrative continues to shape American cultural politics.

Valerie Smith observes that this narrative reemerges in interracial rape cases garnering widespread media attention, even shaping which cases become the focus of attention in the first place. For example, while cases that allege the rape of a white woman by a black man gain widespread notoriety, cases involving the rape of a black woman by a white man rarely receive much attention or investigation.[19] As Smith suggests,

> the explosive coverage of actual or alleged cases of interracial rape (the Tawana Brawley case, the Central Park rape, the Willie Horton case, the Stuart murder case, to name a few) and the political uses to which these incidents have been put, suggest the myriad ways in which the history of slavery and lynching informs the construction of racial and gender relations in contemporary United States culture.[20]

Smith argues that in the above cases, the mainstream media rearticulated and invigorated "myths of black male animalism and of the black male rapist. . . . In terms that recalled lynch law at the turn of the century."[21] More recently, this narrative has informed perceptions of the O. J. Simpson arrest and trial. The darkening of Simpson's face on the cover of a popular magazine reinforced the correlation between blackness and danger, and a Gallup poll commissioned by the *Oprah Winfrey Show* found that 39 percent of white respondents and 43 percent of African American respondents claimed that they would be less interested in the Simpson case if it did not involve an interracial relationship (or, we might surmise, if the man were white and the victim an African American woman).

This narrative that positions the black male as a constant sexual threat is reiterated and manipulated in contemporary white supremacist discourse. The fact that discussion of interracial sexuality in this discourse pivots almost exclusively on this image reveals the staying power of this narrative and fear. As a signifying system of meaning, a photograph of a white woman with an Asian American man, for example, does not have the same symbolic power. The image of interracial sexuality between a white woman and a black man is pregnant with meaning in the American imaginary. Powerful enough to serve as a symbol of all interracial sexuality, it is all the more powerful because it links whatever is being discussed with a whole chain of historical meanings.

The image of interracial sexuality between black men and white women is so powerful that it serves as a metaphor throughout the discourse for not just all interracial sexuality, but all threats to the racial and gender order constructed and supported in the discourse, as we have witnessed. This image is manipulated to not only rationalize violence against people of color, but to justify white supremacy as natural and necessary.

Throughout white supremacist discourse, black male sexuality is described as dangerous and animal-like, a threat to the maintenance of the racial boundary. For example, a photograph published in the *National Vanguard* depicts a black male and white female, nude and embracing. The caption beneath the photograph reads "RACEMIXING: . . . Blacks crave it." The accompanying article asserts, "Lust . . . may be too gentle a word for the maelstrom in the black male's brain."[22] The black male is portrayed as always ready to attack. White supremacist publications are filled with articles about black male crime, especially rapes of white women. Photographs of black men are often published with captions such as "wanted for brutal murder and rape."[23]

The image of interracial sexuality between a black male and white female is predicated not only on this image of the black male, but also on specific constructions of white men, white women, and black women. Interracial sexuality between white women and black men symbolizes the ultimate threat and insult to white masculinity. Interracial sexuality is not only about gender relations between men and women, but between men as well. As Smith reveals,

> instances of interracial rape constitute sites of struggle between black and white men that allow privileged white men to exercise their property rights over the bodies of white women. As Angela Davis has shown, in the United States and other capitalist countries, rape laws, as a rule, were framed originally for the protection of men of the upper classes whose daughters and wives might be assaulted. By this light, the bodies of women seem decidedly less significant than the interests of their male superordinates.[24]

For white supremacists, interracial sexual relations between white women and black men are the ultimate affront to white male power. Contributing to this analysis, Susan Fraiman builds upon Eve Sedgewick's assertion that women mediate erotic relations between men, suggesting that it is also

> important to explore the way women also mediate rivalries between men that cannot be wholly assimilated to "love." In the American

imagination today, women are often at the nexus of male struggles
that, however eroticized, are more fully explained in terms of attempts
both to enforce and to oppose white supremacy.[25]

Fraiman explores a number of sites, including the Central Park jogger rape
case, where narratives about race, gender, and sexuality inform battles between racialized men over the bodies of women. She argues that

> the Central Park jogger case [stands] for one paradigm of American
> racism, available during slavery but crystallized in the period following
> Reconstruction and still influential today, in which white men's control
> of Black men is mediated by the always-about-to-be-violated bodies
> of white women.[26]

Black males are defined as a threat to white women and therefore to white
masculinity and the unrestricted access of white males to white women.
White women are defined as innocent, frail, and passive, always in need of
white male protection. It is white women who are at risk of being seduced
into interracial sexual relationships. For example, a *Thunderbolt* article proclaims, "Let us warn our young White women of the great danger inherent
in socializing with black males."[27] There are no similar warnings for white
men.

In white supremacist discourse, the battle over racial identity is fought
over the bodies of white women. The female body is figured as the passive
turf over which racialized men battle for power. As an *Instauration* article
asserts, it is a

> form of symbolic conquest and triumph over the hated yet desired
> race whose members view him [the nonwhite male] as inferior and
> unworthy. By using one of its female members to serve his desires he
> is striking at the race's soul and degrading it in the most effective
> manner possible.[28]

Interracial sexuality comes to represent not only an attack against the white
race, but one especially against white masculinity. For example, *Crusader*
has published a photograph of a white woman holding her infant. The caption explains, "a beautiful but brainraped white girl attends to her mongrel
offspring, conceived in the abysmal mentality of liberalism."[29] The description of the woman as "brainraped" suggests that she is not acting of her own
free will. White women in interracial sexual relationships are depicted as

literally raped by black men or mentally brainwashed, or "brainraped," by pro-race-mixing propaganda spread by Jews, the media, or feminists. White women are not held responsible for their actions and are instead depicted as in need of protection.

An article in *Instauration* presents a sociobiological argument, describing sexual relations as instinctual. The article suggests that men instinctually seek the most attractive women, i.e., white, while women seek men with power and money who will be able to offer support and security for their offspring. The article argues that while men of all races desire white women, in the past white women mated with white men because they held greater prestige, power, and wealth. This "natural" course of events has been subverted, however, "in a culture where traditional rewards are now bestowed on minorities, [so] the female drive to mate upward is wreaking havoc among the Majority."[30] This article asserts that nonwhite males are now being given the rewards once rightfully reserved for white men, leading white women into the arms of the former. White women, however, are not blamed for choosing nonwhite mates:

> Women cannot be blamed for their overriding concern with power and the men who wield it. Their method of perceiving and reacting to the world is nothing less than a genetically determined survival mechanism. . . . They know that majority males are becoming ever more powerless. So they abandon their race in favor of conditions that promise greater security and greater reproductive success.[31]

White women are viewed as guided by instinct, prisoners of biology. Because they are denied sexual agency, they are not held responsible for their involvement in interracial sexual relations.

Exploring the gendered dimension of the threat of interracial sexuality, a central contradiction emerges: while all interracial sexuality is taboo, there are virtually no discussions of white men and black women (or any women of color). Historically, it has only been the relationship between white women and black men that has been feared; relations between white men and black women have been ignored. In this discourse, the absence of any recognition of the latter relationships highlights the same double standard rooted in slavery. Access to all women characterizes white masculinity, and the relationship between white men and black women is not identified as a threat to white racial identity. Because of the still-present one-drop rule, from a white perspective, black women can only produce black children.

Interracial sexual relationships between white men and black women, therefore, are not seen as contributing to the mongrelization of the race. Additionally, because of the penetration issues, male bodies are not defined as
capable of being polluted in heterosexual relations. There are no theories
proffered to explain the pollution of white male bodies. Homosexuality represents the only threat to white male bodily integrity, partially accounting
for white supremacists' strong hatred of homosexuals.

White supremacist discourse defines black women as promiscuous and
oversexualized, so that rape or coercion of them is ignored by the white
community. Suzanne Harper suggests that black women are less visible in
this discourse, yet at the same time exist as the "antithesis of white
women."[32] Women are characterized exclusively in terms of their sexuality
or reproductive ability, and black women are defined as "prodigious breed-
ers," exuding "wanton and unrestricted" sexuality.[33] The interracial sexual
relations between white men and black women are dismissed along two
contradictory lines. The first defines black women as oversexualized, and
because black women can only give birth to black children, interracial sexuality between white men and black women is not defined as a threat to
whiteness. White women's bodies come to symbolize the white race at risk;
white men's bodies do not.

On the other hand, interracial sexual relations between white men and
black women are totally denied and made to seem unthinkable. Images of
black women in contemporary white supremacist discourse portray them as
inherently unattractive. As pointed out in chapter six, while the beauty of
white women is emphasized throughout the discourse, black women are
always described as ugly. An article in *Instauration* suggests that "the clear-
est proof of this is the consistent use of female Nordics in the worldwide
advertising of consumer products."[34] Harper observes that the implicit message in white supremacist descriptions of black women is that they are inherently unappealing to white men.[35] This discourse therefore makes the
thought of interracial sexual relations between white men and black women
unthinkable, suggesting that no white man would ever choose a black
woman over a white woman.

The narrative of interracial sexuality between white women and black
men highlights the intersections of race and gender relations and is pivotal
to constructing racialized, gendered identities in white supremacist discourse. It serves as a powerful threat and draws its strength from its central-

ity to American history and its repeated rearticulations in contemporary mainstream cultural politics.

NOTES

1. Ridgeway 1990, 90.
2. Anti-Defamation League 1988b.
3. *Elkhart Truth* 1992, 5.
4. *The Thunderbolt* December 1980, 6.
5. *The Thunderbolt* August 1981, 4.
6. *The New Order* March 1979, 1.
7. *The New Order* March 1979, 1.
8. *Instauration* August 1980, 19.
9. *The New Order* March 1979, 2.
10. Butler 1990, 133.
11. *The Thunderbolt* June 1975, 8.
12. *National Alliance Bulletin* December 1978, 4.
13. *The Thunderbolt* February 1982, 9.
14. Butler 1990, 131–32.
15. Young 1995.
16. Gooding-Williams 1993, 4.
17. Gooding-Williams 1993, 4.
18. Baker 1993, 38.
19. Smith 1994.
20. Smith 1994, 157.
21. Smith 1994, 161.
22. *National Vanguard* May 1979, 11.
23. *The Thunderbolt* May 1982, 3.
24. Smith 1994, 158.
25. Fraiman 1994, 69.
26. Fraiman 1994, 71.
27. *The Thunderbolt* no. 297, 3.
28. *Instauration* June 1980, 6.
29. *Crusader* 1979, 9.
30. *Instauration* December 1986, 15.

31. *Instauration* December 1986, 15.
32. Harper 1993, 148.
33. Harper 1993, 149, 156.
34. *Instauration* December 1986, 15.
35. Harper 1993, 156.

8

MONGREL MONSTROSITIES

Mongrelization of the White race is the single greatest danger facing the world today. It is a far greater threat than an atomic attack from Russia or a depression. We could make a comeback from such temporary disasters, but we could never again rebreed the White Race out of interracial mongrels.[1]

Interracial sexuality threatens the borders of white identity, and mixed-race people become the living embodiment of that threat. White supremacist publications are filled with images of "mongrels"—feared and despised because they straddle and destabilize those racial boundaries essential to securing white identity and power.

Gender and race are not identities imposed upon bodies; bodies only become culturally intelligible as they become gendered and racialized. At the same time, however, the regulation of heterosexual and racially pure reproduction produces a domain of abjection, a realm of the culturally unintelligible. As Judith Butler points out, it is

> important to recognize that oppression works not merely through acts of overt prohibition, but covertly, through the constitution of viable subjects and through the corollary constitution of a domain of unviable (un)subjects—abjects, we might call them. . . . Here oppression works through the production of a domain of unthinkability and unnameability.[2]

Throughout this discourse, the realm of abjection includes a number of figures: the mixed-race individual and the Jew, as well as the feminized male

and the masculinized female described by Butler. These figures are produced to safeguard white male hegemony. Each of these figures symbolizes
some wrong identification and serves as an image of boundary confusion
and chaos. The regulation of interracial sexuality, then, is a continuous effort
at boundary maintenance, producing properly racialized and properly gendered subjects as well as this realm of unintelligibility.

THE THREAT TO RACIAL IDENTITY

The properly racialized, gendered subject must repeatedly disassociate
itself from the abject to construct itself as a subject.

> It is this repeated repudiation by which the subject installs its bound-
> ary and constructs the claim to its "integrity." . . . This is not a buried
> identification that is left behind in a forgotten past, but an identifica-
> tion that must be leveled and buried again and again, the compulsive
> repudiation by which the subject incessantly sustains his/her boundary
> . . . subject-positions are produced in and through a logic of repudia-
> tion and abjection.[3]

Figures of abjection are essential to the production of racialized, gendered
subjects. The construction of stable racial identities can only occur in relation to the production and regulation of the impure.

It is through the construction and maintenance of racial boundaries, and
the demarcation of "whiteness" as a racially pure identity, that the white
subject is constructed. While those who are discovered to be of mixed black/
white ancestry are usually defined as black in the United States, they nevertheless represent a potential threat to the construction of racial identity
based on the illusion of white racial purity. More importantly, mixed-race
people signal the instability and permeability of racial boundaries; the regulation of interracial sexuality is required in order to secure the borders.
Blackness, as long as it is carefully separated and subordinated to whiteness,
poses no threat to the existence of a white identity; in fact, blackness is
necessary to the definition of whiteness. White and black form a binary
opposition, and white identity requires its relationship to blackness. Those
who are mixed-race, however, threaten the white/black binary; they signify
the instability of that opposition. Recently mixed-race people have increasingly organized under the banner of mixed-race identity, refusing to accept

the predominant system of single-race categorizations. This development is particularly troublesome for white supremacists. Mixed-race people announce that the boundaries are permeable and put at risk the possibility of a racially pure identity. They threaten the binary opposition itself and the continuation of difference. If subjects only become culturally intelligible in this discourse as they become racialized, mixed-race people cannot be granted subject status; they symbolize the realm of the unlivable, "the very limit to intelligibility."[4]

The production of properly racialized and gendered subjects depends on the power of the threat of racial and gendered punishment, and throughout this discourse that threat emerges again and again. Mixed-race individuals serve as illustrations of racial punishment, figures of abjection. The terms used to refer to these people question their humanity. They are referred to as mongrels, monsters, half-breeds, etc., terms that put in question their humanity. Mongrels do not meet the racialized norm "which qualifies a body for life within the domain of cultural intelligibility."[5] In *The Turner Diaries*, readers are warned,

> The enemy we are fighting fully intends to destroy the racial basis of our existence. No excuse for our failure will have any meaning, for there will be only a swarming horde of indifferent, mulatto zombies to hear it. There will be no White men to remember us.[6]

Not only is race at stake, but what it means to be human. As Michael Omi and Howard Winant and Butler have suggested, the construction of human subjects occurs through the construction and regulation of intelligible racial and gender identities. The above passage suggests that there will be no humans left, only "mulatto zombies." Without a stable racial identity, one can have no human identity in this discourse. Butler explains,

> the "coherence" and "continuity" of "the person" are not logical or analytic features of personhood, but, rather, socially instituted and maintained norms of intelligibility . . . the very notion of "the person" is called into question by the cultural emergence of those "incoherent" . . . beings who appear to be persons but who fail to conform to the gendered [and racialized] norms of cultural intelligibility by which persons are defined.[7]

This incoherence is emphasized in a *New Order* article describing mixed-race individuals as

Malformed pieces of humanity sporting a combination of wooley negroid hair, white complexion and slanted mongol eyes. They call themselves "black people," but they are neither black, white or yellow, but
all and none of these races. These are the children of integration. They
have no culture, no common heritage, no identity and no pride. What
would *you* call them? Half-castes? Hybrids? Monsters?[8]

Mixed-race persons are defined as defective or degenerate, monsterlike;
their humanity is put in question. Similarly, articles in *White Power* refer to
them as "mongrel monstrosities."[9] Interracial sexuality is constructed as a
threat to both racial and human identity, producing *incoherent* beings—
brown zombies.

Mixed-race people are referred to as "negroidal mongrels who on their
own could not build a pyramid or modern city."[10] Elsewhere, we are told
that "a mulatto or mongrel race is a shiftless, lazy, mindless, leaderless and
slave-like race which must have a racial superior 'boss-man' to tell them
what to do."[11] White supremacist discourse suggests that mixed-race people
are inhuman, incapable of surviving on their own or of creating anything
worthwhile. A *New Order* article warns that interracial sexuality will result
in a "race-mixed and totally dead America."[12]

Throughout contemporary white supremacist discourse, in order to exist
as a culturally intelligible being, one must be racialized. To have no pure
race makes living impossible—"mongrels" occupy the realm of impossibility
and unlivability. According to *The New Order*, "a fate worse than death . . .
is what mongrelization is all about. It is a living death."[13]

If white identity is dependent upon racially pure reproduction, and its
place on one side of the binary opposition of white/black, it is essential for
white supremacists to be able to recognize who is white and who is not.
Their own identity depends upon it. In order to engage in racially pure
reproduction and not pollute their own bodies through sexual contact with
nonwhites, it is imperative that whites be able to recognize who is and is not
white. Race is constructed through the reiteration of physical differences
that are visible and knowable, and the existence of mixed-race individuals is
represented as a threat to this surety. In a *National Vanguard* article entitled
"Beware The Almost Whites!" readers are warned that interracial sexuality
produces

a continuous range of mongrels between the two racial extremes. Near
the White end of the spectrum there will be some who . . . will be

almost indistinguishable from the true Aryans. Drawing the line between what is Aryan and what is not becomes more and more difficult.[14]

An article in *The New Order* further explains, "The 'murder by miscegenation' device works all too well when . . . 'almost Whites' . . . can gain acceptance when a nigger cannot."[15] The existence of "almost whites" poses a
threat to the constructed surety of racial identity and symbolizes the insecu-
rity and permeability of racial boundaries, threatening the possibility of racially pure reproduction.

In white supremacist discourse, mongrelization is depicted as leading to
the genocide of the white race. A typical article describes it as "the genocide
of the White race by irreversible downbreeding with a hopelessly inferior
race."[16] Mongrelization, the result of interracial sexuality, is synonymous
with genocide. A National Socialist White People's Party recruitment flyer
accuses, "race-mixing and integration mean White genocide." Mongrelization is equated with genocide because it means the loss of the illusion of
purity upon which whiteness is predicated. As an article in *The Thunderbolt*
explains,

> Mongrelization is the worst form of "genocide." If you kill 99% of a
> race, but leave the other 1% pureblooded, they will in time restore
> the race, but when you mongrelize them, you have destroyed that race
> eternally. Once mixed with the Black or Yellow Races, the White Race
> would be totally and forever destroyed.[17]

Another article asserts, "any large scale intermarriage . . . would mean
the . . . abolition of the White Race. We would simply cease to exist in the
world of the future . . . A race once polluted with the decadent genes of the
lower, backward, and underdeveloped races of the world is lost forever."[18]
White supremacists see race-mixing as even deadlier than outright war because "even a global war in which the Jews were victorious, would leave a
few Whites to breed back the race. Their final solution is MONGRELIZA-
TION. A mongrel can only breed more mongrels."[19] Similarly, a *New Order*
article asserts, "there is one sure way of killing a nation—to destroy or to
fatally dilute the blood of its creators."[20]

If subjects only become living and viable as they become racialized, mongrelization, then, is death. Properly racialized subjects are the only subjects
that qualify for life in this discourse. Interracial sexuality threatens to erase

not only racial difference but the actual continued existence of the white race and humanity.

THE THREAT TO GENDER IDENTITY

Light skin has always garnered privilege in America. E. Franklin Frazier first made this argument, pointing out that mulattoes received advantages denied darker-skinned blacks. Mulattoes were most often house servants and were more likely to be emancipated during slavery by their white fathers, and after slavery they continued to reap the benefits afforded by light skin, achieving higher levels of education and occupational and economic success.[21] Recent work by Kathy Russell, Midge Wilson, and Ronald Hall and Vera M. Keith and Cedric Herring demonstrates that complexion is "more strongly related to stratification outcomes than were such background characteristics as parental socioeconomic status."[22] Keith and Herring conclude that "the effects of skin tone are not only historical curiosities from a legacy of slavery and racism, but present-day mechanisms that influence who gets what in America."[23]

American ideals of female beauty are also based on skin color, and white women have remained the standard. Light skin, straight, smooth hair, and thin features are still the ideal, evident in billboards, magazines, movies, and television.[24] It is no surprise that these ideals are enthusiastically embraced in white supremacist discourse. What is interesting, however, is the way in which these ideals are used in the service of the difference versus equality framework.

Because white female beauty is constructed as a sign of racial difference, interracial sexuality is represented as a threat to that defining feature of whiteness. Interracial sexuality threatens not only racial identity but gender identity. One typical article implores,

> Look at Hawaii today. One-third of all whites marry nonwhites. California is right behind. Remember the "California girl" stereotype of the late '60s? Tall and lean, with blond hair and a tawny body. Well, *Newsweek* ran individual photos of the graduating class at Bakke's medical school in California, and of some 100 students, only five or six had blond hair![25]

Another article provides a fictional account of a white survival demonstration, where protestors chant,

"Sweden is going Brown." "No more Ingrid Bergman." "America is going brown." "No more Cheryl Tiegs." "France is going brown." "No more Catherine Deneuve.". . . "What is the solution?" "White separatism!"[26]

Interracial sexuality is constructed as eliminating difference, making everyone the same inhuman brown, and because white female beauty is defined as a distinguishing feature of whiteness, interracial sexuality is depicted as a threat to that beauty and white aesthetic standards. Readers of white supremacist publications are implored to join the movement to preserve superior white physical features, as figures 6[27] and 7[28] suggest. Images of white children and white women are presented, along with captions such as "Endangered Species." White female beauty, we find, is often used as a measurement to gauge the extent of racial destruction. As summarized elsewhere, "As the race goes, so goes beauty."[29] Another article explains,

Mix these aliens into the population and, sure, you'll still have plenty of individuals with blond hair or with blue eyes or with ultrafine complexions or with classical facial features or with lithe, clean-limbed bodies, but you'll rarely find an individual who combines them all. . . . There won't be any more Greta Garbos. . . . Already in America, there is a frantic male rush after the fast dwindling supply of really Nordic women. You see it all around you in the urban areas and on TV. Today there are hardly enough blonde beauties in all Scandinavia to satisfy the appetites of a few Arab shiekdoms.[30]

Saving the white race is equated not only with saving white female beauty, but with maintaining the sexual availability of white women for white men. The preservation of the white race is refigured as the preservation of white females for the service of white male desire.

In an ongoing debate in *Instauration* about the preservation of Nordic genes, one writer suggests that white sperm be frozen in sperm banks to be brought back in the future when whites are on the brink of extinction. In response, in an article entitled "A Survey of Possible Hiding Places on Earth and Away From Earth: Where to Cache Northern European Genes," the author objects to this self-preservation plan because "while the blondie genes are twiddling their thumbs on the sperm bank shelf, they are not walking around in stuffed shorts and halters to be visually enjoyed."[31] Here, the preservation of the race becomes equated with a voyeuristic desire for preserving white female beauty.

As Anne Flintoff argues, this sexualization of women serves to "reinforce the 'naturalness' of heterosexuality, and a construction of male sexuality based on objectification and conquest."[32] The threat to white female beauty is simultaneously a threat to white male identity and heterosexual gender relations.

Interracial sexuality is posited as a threat to racial differences and, equally importantly, as a threat to white heterosexual gender relations and the fulfillment of white male desire. As another racial warrior warns,

> Believe me, the time is only a few years off when every attractive blonde woman in the world, in Shakespeare's words, may "fall in love with what she feared to look on," and have the chance to marry a dark millionaire.[33]

A threat to one part of the natural order is a threat to the entire natural order. The male/female binary accords males primacy, control, and superiority over the other side of the opposition, females. Male identity is constructed through this opposition: to be a male in this discourse is to have control over women. Interracial sexuality represents the loss of this control. An *Instauration* article, for example, defines that threat:

> When a Northern male sees a female of his race involved in a sexual relationship with a non-Northern male it is evocative, on a racial level and on racial terms, of [what] the male would experience on the individual level upon learning that his wife was being unfaithful to him with another man. The latter is a crime against the individual. The former is a crime against the race . . . to which they are bound by bonds of nature and creation infinitely deeper, stronger and longer-lasting than the mere legal bonds of marriage.[34]

As the above article assumes, white women are considered bound by nature to white males; all white women belong to all white men, and these ties are even greater than the legal ties of marriage. White men have natural rights to white women. The threat to this right is summarized in another article:

> healthy White men are discovering that some of their rightful biological partners are becoming hideous to behold. The skin of these women still gleams like ivory, their bodies as voluptuous as ever. The hideous-

ness comes from the male hand intertwined with one of theirs. The hand is black.[35]

This discourse suggests that interracial sexuality threatens not only to destroy race and human identity, but to destroy gender identity as well. It threatens to destroy what it means to be a man, because what it means to be a man is intimately tied up with race. To be a man is to be a white man who has rights of access to and protects white women. Race and gender identity are absolutely inseparable here; the construction of one depends upon the other. The following excerpt demonstrates this further:

> To further their deracination Northern females are exposed to a culture which is so hostile that films and literature commonly portray Northerners as weak, decadent and degenerate while portraying their non-Northern European counterparts and adversaries as strong and noble. So far has this process gone that non-Northern males are even portrayed as the protectors of Northern females against Northern males, thereby totally usurping the natural role and rights of the Northern male and robbing him of one of his most basic natural functions.[36]

This article, as well as others, asserts that the media's portrayal of interracial sexuality as normal and acceptable behavior, and nonwhite males as the protectors of white women, is a threat to the natural gender order, a threat to the natural role of white men as the protectors of white women.

The breakdown of gender identity and what has been constructed as natural gender relations is frequently represented through images of the improperly gendered. For example, the masculinized female is portrayed as castrating males, assaulting masculinity. These images of gender impropriety are always tied to images of interracial sexuality, reinforcing the notion that a threat to either gender or racial identity is a threat to the other. For example, a *National Vanguard* article depicts

> the castrating female: the militant feminist who wants every male within shrieking distance to know that she is quite capable of taking care of herself and neither needs nor wants any man's support or protection. . . . There are a great many more "liberated" women, who, while not shrill man-haters by any means, through their aggressive assertiveness and their manifest independence tend nevertheless to have a castrating effect on the men in their lives . . . [the husband

whose wife works, even out of economic necessity] feels less a man because of it. . . . All the brave, new talk about marriage today being a partnership of equals does not change the basic, biological natures of men and women. Those natures have fitted them for *complimentary* roles, not for the *same* role. . . . [He is no longer] the master in his house. . . . [In the past,] when a father had some authority over his daughter, and a husband over his wife, another male approached either at his peril. Not only did female dependence carry with it the need for protection, but it also stimulated in the male the desire to provide that protection. The entire community was behind the man who drew his sword or his gun in defense of his womenfolk.[37]

In this article, improperly gendered females are a threat to male identity as well. Any threat to gender hierarchy and white male dominance is an assault upon gender difference and identity and, as described later in this article, leads to interracial sexuality.

Feminists are often depicted as women taking on the characteristics and behaviors attributed to men in this discourse. This gendered boundary confusion is represented as a danger to both gender and racial identity. Additionally, interracial sexuality comes to represent white males' loss of control over white women, putting their masculinity at risk. Images of abject gender go hand in hand with interracial sexuality.

In the last chapter, the articles explored suggested that threats to gender identity and the natural gender order led to interracial sexuality. Here, we see the opposite trajectory: interracial sexuality is depicted as leading to the breakdown of gender relations and gender identity. Racial and gender identities are absolutely intertwined throughout this discourse, and produced through and against the realm of the abject: the improperly raced and gendered. The mongrel symbolizes the breakdown of racial borders; the masculinized female and the feminized male symbolize the breakdown of gender borders. Interracial sexuality is linked to both abject race and gender imagery against which both racialized and gendered subjects are produced. The maintenance of the boundaries that are supposed to prevent interracial sexuality actually produce racialized, gendered subjects.

THE JEW: BOUNDARY MEDIATOR AND DESTROYER

Jews are the imagined masterminds behind this grand plot to race-mix the white race out of existence. Jews are constructed as the ultimate enemy. According to *The New Order*,

The single serious enemy facing the White man is the Jew. The Jews are not a religion, they are an Asiatic *race*, locked in mortal conflict with Aryan man which has lasted for millennia, and which will continue until one of the two combat peoples is extinct.[38]

As *The Thunderbolt* proclaims, it is a "WAR OF EXTERMINATION— God's seed against Satan's seed. ONLY ONE WILL SURVIVE."[39]

Jews are racialized in this discourse. However, according to Christian Identity theology, subscribed to by a number of the publications reviewed here, Jews are not simply different genetically and biologically, but are the children of Satan rather than God.

Christian Identity theology defines Jews as nonwhite and claims that they are not merely a separate race, but an impure race, the product of mongrelization.[40] As explained in an article in *The Thunderbolt* entitled "Satan's Children vs. God's Children," Cain was cast out of Eden and married an "Asiatic" woman.

> His offspring continued mixing with Asiatics, many of whom had previously mongrelized with Negroes, and they continued this miscegenation down through the years. This Cainite line had Satan's spirit, not God's. . . . The genetic function of their existence is to do the works of their father (Satan) by destroying the White Adamic Race. . . . This Cainite race (if you can call mongrels a race) became the people, who today, are known as JEWS . . . over 80% of today's Jews are descendants of the Khazars, who were phallus worshippers before converting to Judaism. . . . Khazars . . . were of Turk-Mongol blood mixed with White Europeans.[41]

Jews are confined to the fate of mongrelization and symbolize all that goes along with that designation. The position of Jews is ambiguous throughout this discourse, because while Jews are defined as mongrels, they are also produced as a distinctive race in a way that mixed-race people more generally are not. Jews are defined as a distinct race, although the product of intermixture, while other mixed-race people are defined as raceless. White supremacists often note that Jews today do not allow intermarriage for themselves. For example, a *Thunderbolt* article explains that

> they are advocating [interracial sexuality] for White Christians and members of the colored races but not for members of the Jew race. . . . They have long realized that the fusion of all the other races (while

maintaining the purity of the Jew race) will produce a race of mongrels more subservient to their domination.[42]

Curiously, Jews are defined as simultaneously mongrels and a pure race. They are produced as a race whose central racial identity *is* impurity, mongrelization, mixture, etc. The pure essence or racial core of the Jew represents all that is antithetical to the meaning of a healthy race in this discourse. According to Zygmunt Bauman, this has traditionally been the role assigned Jews in anti-Semitic discourse:

> The conceptual Jew was a semantically overloaded entity, comprising and blending meanings which ought to be kept apart, and for this reason a natural adversary of any force concerned with drawing borderlines and keeping them watertight. The conceptual Jew was *visquex* (in Sartrean terms), slimy (in Mary Douglas's terms)—an image construed as compromising and defying the order of things, as the very epitome and embodiment of such defiance.[43]

Jews are constructed as symbolizing this site of impossibility and chaos, and the behavior of Jews is described as an extension of that position. Almost every discussion of race-mixing, whether it is school busing or intermarriage, attributes it to Jews. A multitude of articles, found throughout all of the various periodicals, attempts to demonstrate that Jews are responsible for integration and race-mixing. For example, *The Thunderbolt* has published articles with titles like "Jewish Leaders Supporting Race-Mixing," "Jews Finance Race-Mixing Case," "Jewish Organizations Back Interracial Marriage," and "Why Do Jews Support Race-Mixing?"[44] According to the *NSV Report*, Aryans are facing "an organized mutiny of biologically inferior people, led by the Jews against the White race."[45]

Because Jews are consistently presented as the driving force behind integration and race-mixing, it is assumed that if Jews were out of the picture, separation of blacks and whites would be assured. Recalling the articles discussed earlier, we see that blacks are depicted as stupid and apelike, merely following the lead of the Jews, and without the Jews it is believed that blacks would no longer demand equality. Figure 8 provides another stark example: inside the head of the black man is a Jew.[46] The Jew is repeatedly depicted as a puppeteer, controlling the black man's actions.

Instauration articles explain that the Jew serves as the mediator between non-Jewish groups. A book entitled *The Mediator*, by Richard Swartzbaugh, is published by the press that publishes *Instauration*, and *Instauration* articles frequently discuss this book, referred to as an "underground classic." Swartzbaugh

> shows how this mediating role becomes a necessity in cases where mutually antagonistic groups are to be found within the same living space and where some sort of accommodation is desired. That is why the Jews have always done their best artificially to create such situations. However, the mediator's role becomes superfluous when the groups either merge or split asunder irrevocably. Consequently, the Jew would be in danger if a new American populism united the American majority, North and South, farmer and worker.[47]

This work suggests that Jews have always served the role of mediator between races and benefit from and thrive on the breakdown of racial boundaries. Once again, this is seen as Jewish nature—it is part of their racial essence. As an *NSV Report* article explains,

> It is the Jews who are the purveyors of death! Jews are a very negative people. They cannot help it. It is their racial personality. They will destroy your nation, race, culture, civilization, family and whatever you value.[48]

Jews are constructed as a race that by nature disrupts and destroys.

This discourse suggests that the Jew, who symbolizes and embodies the unnatural, the chaotic, and the destruction of the natural order, is disrupting the natural racial order of separation and white superiority and control. As an article in *The Thunderbolt* explains, "When misled liberals and Jews constantly tell negroes that they are equal to (or better) than [*sic*] Whites, hatred and violence erupts when they are unable to compete."[49] While the black man is frequently presented as a dangerous threat, whether as a criminal or rapist of white women, it is often suggested in this discourse that racial order and white male hegemony could be restored if the Jews and their brainwashed white liberals were out of the picture and American society returned to its "natural" racial order of segregation and "old-fashioned justice."

The breakdown of natural racial boundaries is depicted as leading inevitably to interracial sexuality, part of the Jewish plan to exterminate the white race. According to the *NSV Report*, "Jewish parasites . . . race-mix our people into oblivion."[50]

Newsletters often publish cartoons depicting the awesome power and control attributed to Jews, ranging from the media to the banking and finance industries.[51] The United States is often referred to as the "Zionist Occupied Government" (ZOG) or the "Jewnited States." A *White Power* article entitled "Race-Mixing in the Movies" asserts that Hollywood and the motion picture industry were created by, and are controlled by, Jews and have "taken a leading position as a promoter of race-mixing and miscegenation. . . . This medium is now being systematically used to undermine our Aryan values and destroy our White identity."[52] Another article suggests that the "Jew controlled media" is brainwashing children and teens into accepting interracial sexuality and homosexuality so that "White kids see miscegenation and homosexuality portrayed as the 'in' thing, and anyone who opposes this sort of filth is castigated as a 'racist' or a 'prude.' "[53]

The feminist movement is also linked with the Jewish plan to divide the white race and increase interracial sexuality. Jews are considered the driving force behind feminism, "never less than a third of the leadership of feminist organizations."[54] Similarly, a *White Power* article confirms that

> the "Women's Movement" which evolved out of the social turmoil of the 1960s had a distinctly Jewish approach and leadership . . . they seem to be less interested in securing equal rights for women than in turning men and women into unnatural rivals, each struggling against the other for supremacy instead of working together.[55]

Because it is supposedly inherent in Jewish nature to disrupt and threaten difference, Jews are assumed to be behind all movements for racial or gender equality.

Racist publications warn that white genocide and world domination are the end goal of this Jewish conspiracy. A *Thunderbolt* article proclaims

> They hope that our seed will vanish into the Jewish contrived "melting pot" with the negroes, Puerto Ricans, Asians and Mexicans in order to create a brown skinned non-White world of the future. The Jews are waging a fierce battle to stop intermarriage within their own race. If the Jews are the last race able to retain their own racial identity they will be able to use their money power to control any mentally dulled race of mongrelized zombies that might eventually be the majority.[56]

According to a *White Power* article entitled "Jews Planning White Genocide," "world Jewry's chilling Final Solution [is] the physical and spiritual genocide of the White race they despise."[57]

Gendered Punishment

Jews serve as figures of abject racial identity, similar to the mongrel, occupying a site of impossibility and chaos. However, Jews also symbolize abject sexuality and gender confusion. The Jew destabilizes not only racial boundaries, but gender boundaries as well.

Throughout this discourse, Jews represent "unnatural" sexuality. Christian Identity theology establishes Jewish origins among the "phallus" worshiping "Khazars." Jews are also frequently associated with homosexuality. The "rabid sex-perverted Jew"[58] is held responsible for the moral decay of America. Throughout the publications I reviewed, Jews are blamed for the pornography industry, which is characterized as an exploiter primarily of Nordic women. According to *The Thunderbolt*, "90% of the pornography in America is produced by Jew owned businesses."[59] According to *Instauration*, "America's juiciest . . . sex scandals often involve Jews," and these scandals are reported in detail in each newsletter, including stories involving homosexuals, sadists, and the seduction of Aryan women.[60]

The issue of circumcision is also mined to support the charge that Jews are a threat to "normal" sexuality and a particular threat to Aryan men. An article in *Instauration* entitled "Foreskinning" exclaims that "slicing off babies' foreskins cannot be described as anything but forms of mutilation" performed by "savages."[61]

As Butler suggests, the construction of properly gendered subjects occurs through the regulation of heterosexuality and the abjection of homosexuality. In this discourse, Jews are not constructed as properly gendered. They not only occupy the site of abject racial, but gender identity as well. Because they are associated with homosexuality and other forms of "perverse" sexuality, the masculinity of Jewish men and the femininity of Jewish women are put into question. Homosexuality and gender chaos are linked. For example, *Instauration* repeatedly refers to homosexuals as "the third sex."[62] If proper gender positions are assumed through the regulation of heterosexuality, homosexuals in this discourse are not produced as proper males or females. Normal gender identity requires heterosexuality.

Jessie Daniels found that Jewish men are represented as feminizing, whether it be other men or the nation as a whole. An article in *WAR* asserts that "One of the characteristics of nations which are controlled by the Jews is the gradual eradication of masculine influence and power and the transfer of influence into feminine forms."[63] Jewish men are portrayed as feminine and feminizing, and the frequent references to circumcisions implies their castration.

Conversely, caricatures of Jewish women portray them as " 'mannish' or masculinized."[64] One drawing discussed by Daniels depicts "Miss Israel of 1989" with a hairy body and male genitalia. The association of Jewish women with feminism is also used to suggest that Jewish women are aggressive and unfeminine, even antifeminine. As Daniels surmises, there is "no mention of the women's movement that does not make reference to the Jewish leaders of the movement."[65] When Jewish women are discussed in this discourse, it is usually as either feminists or lesbians, who have become synonymous in this discourse. An *Instauration* article claims, "There is an enormous overlap between the American homosexual and feminist movements, in terms of membership, activities, tactics and ideology."[66] The Jewish woman serves as a threat of gendered punishment, representing abject gender and sexuality. An *Instauration* article argues that feminism is motivated by Jewish women jealous of white women's beauty and femininity:

> the leading spokewomen for "feminism" have been—by their own admission—frustrated Jewesses. . . . The entire Jewish tradition has favored mental abstraction over mind-body harmony and instinct for thousands of years—and has actually selected *against* feminine grace—so it is no wonder the Jewesses feel shortchanged in a Nordic country. . . . It isn't America's "macho" males who are under these Jewesses' skins so much as the blonde "shikses." Since they can't beat them in the body department, the Abzugs and Friedans declare the entire sacred domain of fertility/nurture/physical quality to be secondary in life when it should be primary.[67]

The Jewish woman is presented as gender-confused, overly masculine, and (usually) lesbian.

These portrayals have Jewish men and women straddling the boundaries of the male/female binary opposition. Jews are not constructed as properly gendered subjects, but are instead produced as a *threat* to heterosexual relations. For white supremacists, Jewish men and women threaten the natural gender order, putting the masculinity of white men and the femininity of white women at risk. Jews are the ultimate enemy because they destroy the boundaries through which race and gender identities are produced.

These improperly gendered images of Jews serve as figures of abjection, like the mongrel. The Jew and the mongrel represent abject racial identities and serve as threats to enforce properly racialized identities. Similarly, the improperly gendered Jew serves as the " 'threat' that compels the assumption of masculine and feminine attributes."[68] The image of Jews as improperly gendered serves as a threat of the punishment for transgressing racial and gender boundaries and failing to follow the regulations for a racially pure heterosexuality. As Bauman suggests,

> the conceptual Jew performed a function of prime importance; he visualized the horrifying consequences of boundary-transgression. . . . *The conceptual Jew carried a message; alternative to this order here and now is not another order, but chaos and devastation.*[69]

NOTES

1. *The Thunderbolt* January 1979, 12.
2. Butler 1991, 20.
3. Butler 1993a, 114.
4. Butler 1993a, xi–ii.
5. Butler 1993a, 2.
6. Macdonald 1978, 2.
7. Butler 1990, 17.
8. *The New Order* September 1979, 7.
9. *White Power* February 1973, 3.
10. *The Thunderbolt* August 1979, 9.
11. *The Thunderbolt* no. 297, 3.
12. *The New Order* March 1979, 8.
13. *The New Order* Spring 1982, 2.
14. *National Vanguard* August 1979, 5.
15. *The New Order* March 1979, 2.
16. *White Power* March 1972, 4.
17. *The Thunderbolt* 25 April 1975, 10.
18. *The Thunderbolt* 30 May 1975, 8.
19. *The Thunderbolt* January 1974, 10.
20. *The New Order* March 1979, 2.
21. Frazier 1957; Keith and Herring 1991; Russell, Wilson, and Hall 1992.

22. Keith and Herring 1991, 777.
23. Keith and Herring 1991, 777.
24. Russell, Wilson, and Hall 1992.
25. *Instauration* January 1980, 14.
26. *Instauration* June 1980, 18.
27. *White Power* December 1980, 9.
28. *National Vanguard* May 1978, 1.
29. *Instauration* November 1980, 19.
30. *Instauration* January 1980, 14.
31. *Instauration* June 1980, 14.
32. Flintoff 1993, 83.
33. *Instauration* January 1980, 14.
34. *Instauration* June 1980, 8.
35. *National Vanguard* May 1979, 11.
36. *Instauration* June 1980, 8.
37. *National Vanguard* January 1983, 17.
38. *The New Order* March 1979, 3.
39. *The Thunderbolt* January 1974, 10.
40. Barkun 1994.
41. *The Thunderbolt* January 1974, 10.
42. *The Thunderbolt* no. 297, 3.
43. Bauman 1989, 39.
44. *The Thunderbolt* no. 297, 1; *The Thunderbolt* no. 297, 3.
45. *NSV Report* April/June 1983, 5.
46. *The Thunderbolt* June 1975, 8.
47. *Instauration* April 1979, 28.
48. *NSV Report* January/March 1989, 1.
49. *The Thunderbolt* August 1979, 8.
50. *NSV Report* October/December 1988, 2.
51. *Crusader*, Special Introductory Sampler Issue, 3.
52. *White Power* June/July 1969, 3.
53. *White Power* February 1973, 3.
54. *National Vanguard* January 1983, 17.
55. *White Power* no. 105, 4.
56. *The Thunderbolt* January 1974, 7.
57. *White Power* February 1973, 3.
58. *The Torch* July 1977, 4.
59. *The Thunderbolt* no. 301, 6.

60. *Instauration* February 1982, 21.
61. *Instauration* December 1979, 17.
62. *Instauration* vol. 2, no. 3(February)13.
63. *WAR* vol. 8, no. 2(1989)14 in Daniels 1997, 112–13.
64. Daniels 1997, 116.
65. Daniels 1997, 117.
66. *Instauration* March 1984, 9.
67. *Instauration* June 1984, 16.
68. Butler 1993, 102.
69. Bauman 1989, 39.

9

SECURING THE BORDERS

We do not need complicated political or theological dissertations to "justify" our cause. There is a higher Law, the highest Law. The first Law of Nature is the preservation of your own kind. . . . WE MUST SECURE THE EXISTENCE OF OUR PEOPLE AND A FUTURE FOR WHITE CHILDREN.[1]

Maintaining the existence of the white race in this discourse requires the preservation of difference through the maintenance of racial and gender boundaries. What is presented as the preservation of whiteness is, as we have seen, the *production* of whiteness. Faced with tenuous and vulnerable borders, the white supremacist goal is to secure these boundaries and guarantee white male domination.

PUNISHING TRANSGRESSORS

The threat of interracial sexuality must be eliminated if white supremacy is to be secured once and for all. The threat posed by interracial sexuality to the construction of race, gender, and human identity is considered so great that one organization's attempt to define a "white sexual ethic" declares that *"if anyone lie with one not of his race, then he shall be taken from his house and cast into a pit, and everyone shall stone him until he is dead."*[2]

Death is defined as the only appropriate punishment for interracial sexuality. According to *The Turner Diaries*, in the final stages of the white revolution the threat of miscegenation must be eliminated, and total racial separation must be established. All who have transgressed racial boundaries, the impure and polluted, must be punished. As Turner narrates, this is accomplished during

> the Day of the Rope—a grim and bloody day, but an unavoidable one . . . from tens of thousands of lampposts, power poles, and trees throughout this vast metropolitan area the grisly forms hang. . . . The first thing I saw in the moonlight was the placard with its legend in large, block letters: "I defiled my race." Above the placard leered the horribly bloated, purplish face of a young woman, her eyes wide open and bulging, her mouth agape. . . . There are many thousands of hanging female corpses like that in this city tonight, all wearing identical placards around their necks. They are the White women who were married to or living with Blacks, with Jews, or with other non-White males.[3]

Note that there is no reference here to white males involved in interracial relationships.

A WHITE HOMELAND

In *West of Everything*, Jane Tompkins suggests that "Fear of losing his identity drives a man west."[4] That characterization similarly describes contemporary white supremacist men. Feeling as though both their masculinity and racial identity are at risk, white supremacists also seek to head west, to create a new, white homeland where they can once again be men.

Every white supremacist organization desires the reestablishment of racial segregation, and in order to prevent future threats of integration, they desire some form of geographical separation. The founding of a white homeland is a central concern for many white supremacists. The world is presented as a place where whites have no safe haven to reproduce racially pure children without the threat of pollution. As an *Instauration* article explains,

> Their race [black] will soon be a far higher percentage of the world's population than ever before in historic times. But again, that's not what's most important. What's vital is that virtually all of these blacks will be in countries where nearly 100% of the population is black. Their racial future is assured. If you see a black and a white walking

arm-in-arm, you'd better realize that it poses no threat whatsoever to black survival. Only in America and Brazil are large numbers of blacks integrated. But Northern Europeans almost *everywhere* are already living in racial checkerboards.[5]

Expressing similar anxiety, another article suggests that

the last reasonably autonomous white community broke up somewhere in the Midwest in the early 1970s. This is a profound revolution; the world has never seen its like. It has very little to do with the black man rising . . . rather *it is about the white man falling.*[6] (my italics)

The language used here is part of a broader effort to remake the image of the movement. Rather than be seen as haters, white supremacists attempt to present themselves simply as defenders of the white race.

This discourse proposes the necessity of white separation in order to preserve white difference—it is the only way to save the white race from extinction. An *Introduction to the Knights of the Ku Klux Klan* pamphlet asserts that the Klan is not "the enemy of the Negro race. The only way both races can develop their full potential and culture is through racial separation." Within the framework of the white/black binary opposition, whiteness is constructed through the maintenance of the boundary between the two. The potential collapse of the boundary is a threat to the existence of whiteness. The assertion of the boundary is at the same time the construction of a white identity.

Boundary construction is contested throughout white supremacist discourse. Just as there is a great amount of discussion and argument over what constitutes whiteness, there is much debate over where and how to construct geographical racial boundaries. For example, the National States Rights Party, publisher of *The Thunderbolt*, proposes the "NSRP Official Program For Deporting Negroes 'Back To Africa.'"[7] And the *Western Guardian* supports

Geographical Apartheid—the expulsion of all non-Whites from Western nations . . . [and] A Pure Western Culture and Society—the elimination of non-Western influences from the culture and society of Western nations and the restoration of a healthy interest in and love of the achievements of White Western man.[8]

Other white supremacists, however, support dividing up the United States into racial segments. For example, the *National Association for the*

Advancement of White People's News published a divided map of the United States. This "Proposed Geographical Relocation and Regrouping of America's Unassimilable Minorities" establishes a "White Bastion" in the Northwest, "Navahona" in the Southwest for Native Americans, "Alta California" as a home for Mexican Americans, "New Africa" in the South for "Negroes," "West Israel" on Long Island and Manhattan for Jews, and "Minoria" in the rest of New York for "Puerto Ricans, southern Italians, Greeks, Mediterraneans and other 'unassimilable minorities.' "[9] As the *NSV Report* proclaims, "All White Nationalists . . . want an all-White nation, however there is some disagreement among White Nationalists themselves just how this should be done." The article summarizes an argument that erupted: "One side felt that the best we could do is section up the country, giving each identifiable race an autonomous area of its own. . . . The other side" argued for "repatriation of all non-Whites (except American Indians)."[10] Other disagreements arise regarding the fate of Jews. The NAAWP map provides a geographical area for Jews, yet most publications warn that the white race will never be safe until every last Jew is eliminated from the face of the earth.

The project of creating racial homelands necessarily runs into the problem of defining what constitutes a race and who counts as white. In drawing geographical boundaries, different organizations construct different numbers of races. Most publications, however, support geographical separation as a necessary means of preserving racial difference and identity. As a typical article explains,

> Racism is a natural and healthy instinct instilled by genetic inheritance
> in normal people, regardless of race. A program of total geographic
> separation of the races is a form of racism in which all people are with
> their own races and there is no hate involved.[11]

Here, the separation of races is the natural extension of biological and/or god-given racial differences and the only avenue to prevent mongrelization and reify racial differences. As a *White Patriot* article asserts

> our race and all others should have the right to determine their own
> destiny through self-determination and rule. . . . Every people on this
> planet must have the right to life: the continued existence of its unique
> racial fabric and resulting culture.[12]

WANTED: REAL MEN

Clearly gender is central to the project of constructing whiteness. Consequently, the reestablishment of racial boundaries and the reassertion of a white identity also require the reestablishment of gender boundaries and the reassertion of traditional gender identities. I have argued that the assertion of a white male identity is the central project of white supremacist discourse.[13] If the demasculinization of white males has led to interracial sexuality, then remasculinization is necessary. Contrasting today's attitude with the "healthy Aryan" attitude of earlier times, a *White Power* article offers an example of the

> high esteem which women enjoyed among the ancient Aryans. . . . It stands on record that armies already wavering and on the point of collapse have been rallied by the women, pleading heroically with their men, thrusting forward their bosoms, and making them realize the imminent prospect of enslavement—a fate which the Germans fear more desperately for their women than for themselves.[14]

White masculinity is equated with the desire to protect the women of the race, and interracial sexuality becomes a sign of the demasculinization of white males.

Jessie Daniels contends that

> Since "race-mixing" is tantamount to racial treason, white men, given their representations as racial warriors, martyrs, and heroes, are presumed to be above such sexual betrayals to their racial identity. White women, however, are not immune to such sexually inspired racial disloyalty.[15]

My research refutes that characterization, however. Throughout the publications reviewed here, white men are held responsible for betraying both their racial and gender identity in depictions of their demasculinization and refusal to protect white women and, consequently, the race. While it is true that white men are never depicted engaging in interracial sexuality, we have seen that they are clearly held accountable for much of the interracial sexuality between white women and black men. Another example is found in a *National Vanguard* photograph of a black man and white woman, nude from the waist up, embracing. The caption beneath the photograph reads, "SHAME of White men is their loss of control over their women. This German girl is one of thousands who have sought sexual fulfillment with blacks in Jamaica."[16] Suggesting that white men have failed to hold on to their women, white women are depicted as being forced to turn to black men for sexual fulfillment. Threatening both the masculinity and sexuality of white men, the pornographic photograph also suggests what the white man *could* have if he asserts his masculinity: the seminude white woman is held out as a reward for the real white man.

Throughout white supremacist discourse, various strategies are employed to provoke male readers to embrace white supremacy. Like Judith Butler, Michael S. Kimmel argues that gender is tied to sexuality. We frequently assume that we can " 'read' one's sexual orientation through the successful performance of gender identity."[17] Questioning a man's sexuality, then, is a pointed way of attacking his masculinity. "Homophobia is a central organizing principle of our cultural definition of manhood," Kimmel continues. "Homophobia is the fear that other men will unmask us, emasculate us, reveal to us and the world that we do not measure up, that we are not real men."[18] Verbal put-downs that question or insult men's masculinity are commonly used as an "identity-building" strategy. The ultimate insult to a male suggests that he is feminine and "girly," or questions his heterosexuality. Anne Flintoff found that "using women and homosexuals as negative reference groups" encouraged men to distance "themselves from any behaviour or activity associated with femininity."[19] This threat is commonly employed in white supremacist discourse, primarily through the figures of abject gender and sexuality previously discussed.

In numerous other articles white masculinity is directly attacked. Contemporary white American men are described as effeminate. A *National Vanguard* article warns that

> As Northern males have continued to become more wimpish, the result of the media-created image of the "new male"—more pacifist, less authoritarian, more "sensitive," less competitive, more androgynous, less possessive—the controlled media, the homosexual lobby, and the feminist movement have cheered . . . the number of effeminate males has increased greatly—not just the sexual inverts, who actually have taken pseudo-female sexual roles, but even more the legions of sissies and weaklings, of flabby, limp-wristed, non-aggressive, non-physical, indecisive, slackjawed, fearful males who, while still heterosexual in theory and practice, have not even a vestige of the old *macho* spirit, so deprecated today, left in them.[20]

The attack on white masculinity is once again made through relation to the realm of the abject. Males are threatened with castration, demasculinization, and the accusation of homosexuality.

The threat of demasculinization and homosexuality compels the assumption of properly gendered positions and is used in this discourse to align properly gendered positions with white supremacy. Male readers' masculinity is frequently assaulted in order to invite them to become "real men" by joining the white supremacist movement. As Kimmel argues, men

> are under constant careful scrutiny of other men. Other men watch us, rank us, grant our acceptance into the realm of manhood. Manhood is demonstrated for other men's approval. . . . Masculinity is a *homosocial* enactment. We test ourselves, perform heroic feats, take enormous risks, all because we want other men to grant us our manhood.[21]

Kimmel's insights are particularly helpful for understanding white supremacist discourse. For example, there are frequent articles that describe "The whimpering collapse of the blond male."[22] Insulting the "manhood" of white males is employed as a means of provoking them to action. For example, an article in *Instauration* is designed to incite masculinity and violence by insulting white manhood. Musing over the declining numbers of whites, the author writes that

> it'd be nice to keep a few of the beautiful blond women around, but not if it means we must endure for another day the cowardly whimperings of their menfolk . . . if they do not regain their manhood, then let them have a quick demise.[23]

Suggesting that the loss of masculinity and the failure of white manhood is responsible for the decline of the race, the author then ridicules Klan violence, writing

> For hate, that is small potatoes, nowhere near enough to save any race that has let itself be integrated the world over. . . . At the same time those Nordics down in Alabama were lighting a candle—I mean a cross—against busing, not so many miles away a big angry mob of Mexicans was invading their country in broad daylight—without hoods or sheets.[24]

The actions of Mexican immigrants are refigured as an attack and invasion of white territory and read as an assertion of nonwhite masculinity. The actions of the Klan, on the other hand, are figured as meek and cowardly displays, insulting the masculinity of its members.

Articles frequently imply that the men of other races are acting more like "real men" than white men. An article about black Jamaican men explains,

> It is their unabashed sensuality, their wildness, their readiness to fight over any affront to what they think of as their manly dignity, their arrogant flaunting of their maleness which lure the civilized but male-hungry women of the decadent, effeminate West to them.[25]

This article attacks the masculinity of white men and suggests that their racial counterparts are more masculine. Figures 9a and 9b accompany this article and depict bare-chested, muscular, black Jamaican men, set in a junglelike setting. The caption reads

> RASTAFARIANS consciously cultivate an image of Black Tarzans in order to attract White women. They emphasize not only the physical masculinity that so many flabby white-collar White males lack, but also a primitive life-style that suggests the more natural relationship that existed between the sexes in earlier times.[26]

This "unnatural" feminization of white men is blamed for leading to interracial sexuality between white women and black men, because white men cannot hold on to their women. Black men are depicted as seducing white women by asserting a natural masculinity, one in which men control and master women. Making a similar point, a *White Power* article warns that

> attacks, beatings, rapes and TORTURE KILLINGS OF WHITE PEOPLE—has been nothing but the manifestation of a steadily escalating anti-White guerrilla campaign. . . . Lincoln Rockwell once predicted that in the coming race war, a man's uniform would be the color of his skin. The Blacks understand this perfectly—and they're acting accordingly. Only the White man—brainwashed by years and years of "love and brotherhood" propaganda—is a helpless sitting duck in the battle for survival which has begun.[27]

The fate of the white race hinges on the need for real white men to act.

Kimmel argues that the "fear of being seen as a sissy dominates the cultural definitions of manhood," and leads to shame and silence. For example, that "furtive silence when men make sexist or racist jokes in a bar. That clammy-handed silence when guys in the office make gay-bashing jokes.

Our fears are the sources of our silences, and men's silence is what keeps the system running."[28] This insight is profound, and helps us to understand why men often refuse to question inequality. We can take this insight further, however. Shame not only leads to silence, it leads to action. It is this same shame that compels those men who make those sexist, racist, and homophobic jokes. And it may be this same shame that compels men to join the white supremacist movement in the hope of securing and proving, once and for all, their masculinity.

The white supremacist movement attacks white masculinity, and argues that this is the source of all of our problems today. As a *New Order* article suggests, "the world is in trouble now only because the White man is divided, confused and misled. Once he is united, inspired by a great ideal and led by real men, his world will again become livable, safe and happy."[29] The white supremacist project is primarily concerned with reaffirming white men's masculinity. The white supremacist movement offers itself as the solution—white men may regain their rightful position as patriarchs by joining the movement. As a recruitment pamphlet for the Knights of the Ku Klux Klan explains, "*The KKK is a fraternal movement*. We are actually building today our new Community of White racial brotherhood."

The vision of masculinity forged within this discourse attempts to bridge class lines. Class differences are frequently characterized as just another Jewish tool to divide the white race. For example, the *New Order* explains that "National Socialism utterly refutes and denounces the false concept of 'class struggle' which pits White property owners against White workers in another version of [the] Jewish 'divide and conquer' scheme."[30] Elsewhere, readers are warned that " 'Capitalist' or 'Communist': both divide the people of the world into economic classes, as if material bondage were stronger than an ancient, collective racial soul."[31]

Class differences are recast as the product of racial conflict. Class differences are depicted as illusory, constructed to draw attention away from what are considered the true differences. White supremacist recruitment efforts often target "deserving White poor people who are bypassed by the minority-oriented social programs of government and large foundations."[32] This discourse posits class as the product of a Jewish-controlled economy that benefits minorities through social programs, like welfare and affirmative action, and aims to divide and destroy the white race. White men are depicted as victims of class oppression by virtue of their race, and sometimes gender. The white supremacist project offers a vision of an alternative society where all whites will be economically secure. For example, as a typical article suggests,

> It is our RACE we must preserve, not just one class. . . . White Power
> . . . means a permanent end to unemployment because, with the non-
> Whites gone, the labor market will no longer be over-crowded with
> unproductive niggers, spics and other racial low-life. It means an end
> to inflation eating up a man's paycheck faster than he can raise it be-
> cause OUR economy will not be run by a criminal pack of interna-
> tional Jewish bankers, bent on using the White worker's tax money in
> selfish and even destructive schemes.[33]

Readers are often warned in the pages of these newsletters to prevent class differences from interfering with the goals of a united white race. For example, *The National Alliance Bulletin* warns its members that "a conscientious effort will be required of all members to avoid allowing socioeconomic differences to give rise to attitudes which threaten harmonious collaboration in the performance of the Alliance's task."[34]

The reassertion of masculinity is construed as essential to reasserting the power and identity of whiteness and protecting the race and its women. This is further demonstrated by figure 10. A drawing of a Nazi stormtrooper is displayed next to the photographs of an interracial couple and a black man raising his fist as a symbol of black power. Next to these pictures, the caption reads: "ONLY THE STORMTROOPER CAN STOP THIS."[35] According to this discourse, only white supremacists, the only "real men," can stop interracial sexuality and return white women to white men. In this discourse, to be a white supremacist is to be a real man. The *White Patriot* announces: "To Be A Klansman . . . You come as a man, to be among men."[36] This vision of masculinity revolves around the protection of white women and the race. An *Instauration* author describes this vision:

> I have dreamt of a New Man . . . aware of who he is. . . . He is not a
> member of a "human race" that does not exist, but of one of the races
> making up humanity. . . . He is strong, proud. He knows beauty and
> loves it. He is something high, a man. *And he is a ruthless animal.*
> When he or his kind are threatened, he will spring upon the Enemy
> with a ferocity unmatched by any lower beast. Not cruelly, but swift
> destruction shall be his purpose. Respecting all life, he nonetheless
> respects *his* and his *kind* most of all.[37]

Masculinity is defined as a willingness to protect the race at any cost. Similarly, but not quite so eloquently, an NSWPP recruitment flyer featuring a photograph of a Nazi rally explains in the caption, "They've seen the niggers chasing after White chicks. They know about the thousands of White girls (their racial sisters) who are gangraped by apes every year." Male readers are encouraged to join to protect their "White chicks." This is further demonstrated by a comic strip entitled "ARYANMAN Battles the Bestial Hordes of Juda!" Aryanman, "the last man of his race in mongrelized America," is captured by Jews, who have also captured the last white woman. Juda tells Aryanman

> A beauty, yes? Your race had many such women, Aryanman, but your men let us buy them or the negro take them. The white man was turned into a spineless jellyfish by our propaganda machine—this was the real downfall of your race—the men would not fight for their women![38]

Declaring himself a National Socialist and proving himself a "real man," Aryanman fights back. Discovering the existence of a real man, Aryanwoman is given the hope and strength to fight back also. In the end, Aryanman proclaims, "now that there's two of us, there's hope! Perhaps with the grace of God we can help make up for our people who let themselves be mongrelized by the Jew."[39] This comic strip asserts that the failure of white men to defend white women has been the downfall of the race. White men are not portrayed as outraged bystanders, but as failures. White women are absolved of any responsibility for interracial sexuality in this discourse. As this comic strip points out, white women are *sold* to Jews or *stolen* by black men. In contrast to the images of strong and independent women asserted over the last three decades, white women in this discourse are constructed as passive and denied agency. Women cannot be recognized as having control over their own sexuality in this discourse. If women have the power to choose their sexual partners, what then? What if white women are not simply brainwashed or kidnapped? This possibility is refused.

It is white men who must be blamed for allowing their women to be taken from them, "their rightful biological partners." White women are denied control over their own bodies and their sexuality. The only place it is suggested white women have some power is in discussions of white women's birth rates. It is feared that white women are not producing enough white children, and they are implored to reproduce for the race. Figures 11[40] and

12[41] emphasize this point. Even in these images, however, white women are not attacked, and it is unclear whether white women are really blamed. In conjunction with the other images we have explored, the discourse implies that white men should regain control in their relationships, and that decisions regarding numbers of children should not be left to women.

The white female body comes to represent the white race at risk, and the assertion of white masculinity is equated with the protection of the race via the bodies of white women. The protection of "their" women and the race becomes synonymous. It is men who act in this discourse, and white women are the figurative and literal territory over which the race war is waged. "Women become a kind of currency that men use to improve their ranking on the masculine social scale."[42]

The construction of whiteness requires the construction and maintenance of racial and gender boundaries. In order to secure white male privilege and power, the white supremacist project advocates punishing boundary transgressors, constructing geographical borders between races, and producing "real men" who protect their women and the race.

NOTES

1. *NSV Report* July/September 1990, 2.
2. *National Vanguard* August 1982, 16.
3. Macdonald 1978, 160–61.
4. Tompkins 1992, 47.
5. *Instauration* January 1980, 14.
6. *Instauration* February 1980, 14.
7. *The Thunderbolt* 20 June 1975, 10.
8. *The Western Guardian* April 1980.
9. *National Association for the Advancement of White People's News* December 1984, reprinted in Ridgeway 1990, 150–51. David Duke, founder of the NAAWP, claims that this map was originally published in *Instauration*, and that the NAAWP reprinted it as a joke.
10. *NSV Report* October/December 1988, 2.
11. *NSV Report* January/March 1991, 2.
12. *White Patriot* no. 56, 6.
13. Ferber 1995b, 1998a.
14. *White Power* no. 105, 4.

15. Daniels 1997, 125.
16. *National Vanguard* January 1983, 17.
17. Kimmel 1994, 129.
18. Kimmel 1994, 131.
19. Flintoff 1993, 81.
20. *National Vanguard* January 1983, 17.
21. Kimmel 1994, 128–29.
22. *Instauration* February 1980, 14.
23. *Instauration* February 1980, 13.
24. *Instauration* February 1980, 13.
25. *National Vanguard* January 1983, 17.
26. *National Vanguard* January 1983, 21.
27. *White Power* November 1972, 4.
28. Kimmel 1994, 131.
29. *New Order* March 1979, 8.
30. *The New Order* March 1979, 3.
31. *The New Order* Spring 1982, 4.
32. *White Patriot* no. 56, 7.
33. *The New Order* March 1979, 8.
34. *National Alliance Bulletin* October 1979, 3.
35. *White Power* September 1973, 6.
36. *White Patriot* no. 60, 5.
37. *Instauration* April 1981, 13.
38. *White Power* February 1973, 6.
39. *White Power* February 1973, 6.
40. *White Power* no. 101, 1.
41. *White Power* no. 101, 3.
42. Kimmel 1994, 129.

10

NO FINAL SOLUTIONS

When Earl Turner saw a racially mixed couple on the street, the sight did more than arouse a twinge of xenophobia or offend his sense of beauty. Unlike your average voter, he saw all the implications of that mixed couple. He saw mongrel children and mongrel grandchildren; he saw a race defiled. More than that, he saw the whole meaning of life, of existence, thwarted. He saw a threat not just to himself, but to the whole upward course of life; a threat not just to his race, but to what his race could become.[1]

The threat of interracial sexuality functions as a core theme in white supremacist discourse, symbolizing the erasure of racial and gender differences and white male power defined as rooted in nature. Because subjects are constructed in this discourse through the processes of racialization and gendering, the threat to race and gender is also a threat to life itself. The production of culturally intelligible racialized, gendered subjects occurs in relation to the realm of the abject—populated by homosexuals, mongrels, Jews, and the improperly gendered. The construction of essentialized race and gender identities are necessary to the maintenance of hierarchical social relations and are invested with so much meaning that they must be secured and defended with violence. George Lipsitz refers to this process as the possessive investment in whiteness.[2] This investment, however, is threatened by interracial sexuality and must be regulated to ensure the production of racialized, gendered subjects.

While it is currently trendy to study and teach racial diversity, this approach often uncritically reinforces the assumption of inherent racial differences and fails to interrogate the relations of power that construct and maintain them. As bell hooks suggests in *Yearning: Race, Gender, and Cultural Politics*, too often the focus on difference devolves into a celebration of diversity "that fails to ask who is sponsoring the party and who is extending the invitations."[3] She maintains that amidst this environment, a sustained interrogation of whiteness is needed. Attention to whiteness shifts the emphasis from diversity to the relations of power and privilege that construct and maintain racial identities. While it has been a struggle for white scholars to address the oppression of Others, it has taken far longer for white scholars to address white power and privilege. As hooks reflects,

> In far too much contemporary writing . . . race is always an issue of Otherness that is not white; it is black, brown, yellow, red, purple even. Yet only a persistent, rigorous, and informed critique of whiteness could really determine what forces of denial, fear, and competition are responsible for creating fundamental gaps between professed political commitment to eradicating racism and the participation in the construction of a discourse on race that perpetuates racial domination.[4]

Similarly, Patricia J. Williams argues that "one reason that conversations about race are so often doomed to frustration is that the notion of whiteness as 'race' is almost never implicated."[5] In response to these critiques, this book attempts to redirect our attention to the production of whiteness and racial privilege.

While many scholars have noted that whiteness often masquerades as a neutral, colorless, unmarked category,[6] white supremacist politics, on the other hand, explicitly marks whiteness. White supremacists seek to label, define, and demarcate whiteness, providing whites with a history, identity, and superior essence. In the current context where more and more people are coming to see whites as the targets of discrimination—victims of practices like "reverse racism"—white supremacists have adopted the language historically used by oppressed minorities. White supremacists choose to mark whiteness in order to establish the perception that whites face discrimination and are an "oppressed majority." Ironically, white supremacist publications even translate the often unmarked nature of whiteness, a sign of privilege, into a sign of their oppression, arguing that their history and identity have been denied them.

Charles Gallagher discovered a similar phenomenon in his study of backlash among white college students. He concludes that "the perception that a racial double standard exists on campus is commonplace . . . [and] provide[s] the foundation for a white identity based on the belief that whites are now under siege."[7] Numerous scholars have observed that historically, the construction of a white racial identity served to consolidate power and privilege. Noel Ignatiev and John Garvey, for example, argue that "people were not favored socially because they were white; rather they were defined as 'white' because they were favored. Race itself is a product of social discrimination."[8] Whiteness remained invisible as long as white privilege was secure. Indeed, this racial invisibility is itself a privilege.[9] In the current climate, however, many whites believe that they have lost their privileged status and instead become victims of racial discrimination, embracing a strategy of rearticulating whiteness to reclaim privilege.

White supremacist discourse operates to make certain meanings legitimate and others impossible. A poststructuralist discourse analysis has enabled us to move beyond mere description of white supremacist ideology to explore *how* meaning works in this discourse, within the difference versus equality framework. An analysis of the way this framework constructs meaning reveals a series of equations: interracial sexuality is equated with genocide; the civil rights and the women's movements become equated with interracial sexuality and therefore genocide; threats to racial difference are equated with threats to gender difference; interracial sexuality is equated with an assault on white masculinity, etc. Understanding how meaning operates in this discourse is essential to respond more effectively to white supremacy.

This approach also further politicizes the sociological project, highlighting the role of the sociologist in producing reality. In *Nazis, Communists, Klansmen, and Others on the Fringe,* John George and Laird Wilcox argue that "extremism is more an issue of style than of content."[10] The white supremacist movement is usually defined as extremist because of its violent tactics. A resultant problem, however, is that in labeling the movement extremist, the content of its ideas, desires, and goals is also uncritically dismissed as extremist and often go unexplored. Defining the white supremacist movement as an extremist movement, the "fringe" in relation to the mainstream "fabric" of America, defines the mainstream as nonracist in relation to the racism of the fringe. This discursive construction erases from view and diminishes the significance of mainstream racism, rooted in American culture and institutions. This approach defines racism as something rooted in the personality of extremist psychopaths, so that unless they parade around in white hoods, average Americans can say that they are not racists. According to this view, one either is or is not a racist. By abjecting the racism within us, white privilege remains unexamined.

In contrast, we have explored the intersections of race and gender in narratives about interracial sexuality in one site, highlighting the continuity of this narrative with traditional American narratives about interracial danger. The way we define and read the white supremacist movement is a political act with consequences for how we view race and racism. The meaning of these discourses is not given, but constructed for various purposes, and it would be a mistake to assume static consequences of these efforts at linedrawing. While not ignoring or erasing the differences between far right and mainstream, questioning this catgorization can evoke new understandings of both the far right and mainstream. Rather that legitimating far right ideology, I hope to delegitimate mainstream racial discourses that are often not recognized as racist because they congregate under the banner of "mainstream." I have sought to demonstrate that an exploration of white supremacist discourse can also teach us something about our own conceptions of race and gender.

This is especially important if we are interested in organizing against far right violence. In *Reflecting Black: African American Cultural Criticism*, Michael Eric Dyson argues that while we may be tempted to view acts of racial violence as isolated from other manifestations of racism, "its logic and life are sustained" throughout mainstream culture.

> What happened in Bensonhurst, and in Howard Beach before it, is the conspicuous harvest of the seeds of bigotry sown in a thousand insidiously subtle gestures of racial antagonism, insensitivity, and resentment. Our task, in formulating strategies of resistance, is to understand the relationship between the two racisms.[11]

Understanding the relationship between the two racisms means recognizing that the racism of the far right is produced by the mainstream. Most racist violence is not performed by white supremacist organizations, and these groups often attract individuals who are already racist.[12] In expelling the far right from the mainstream, we fail to recognize that members of the far right are nurtured *by* the mainstream. If racism were not cultivated by the mainstream, there could be no far right. Carole Sheffield contends that "hate violence is neither accidental nor coincidental. It is the result of acquired beliefs, stereotypes, expectations . . . based on what the perpetrators of such violence often feel is a betrayal of what they were taught to expect."[13] In other words, it is impossible to dismiss mainstream racism and focus on eliminating the racism of the far right, because the far right can neither be understood nor halted without addressing the mainstream. The far right and mainstream have a reciprocal relationship: they feed upon and back into each other.

We should view the white supremacist movement within a continuum of racist and sexist backlash. As the Anti-Defamation League points out in their analysis of the Skinhead problem, "In those instances where the Skins have had a major impact, it is largely because their views were shared by a broader segment of the population."[14] Contemporary American society has witnessed a wide-ranging backlash to the civil rights, women's, and gay and lesbian movements that have challenged traditional notions of race, gender and sexual identity, and hierarchy. Certainly the white supremacist movement comprises only one small part of this broad-based backlash, manifest in attacks on affirmative action, welfare, bilingual education, immigrant rights, homosexual rights, and the birth of a reactionary men's movement, which includes organizations like the Promise Keepers.

A 1986 Harris poll of Iowa and Nebraska residents found that 27 percent agreed that "farmers have always been exploited by international Jewish bankers who are behind those who overcharge them for farm equipment or jack up the interest on their loans."[15] Even worse, almost half of all respondents agreed that Jews "should stop complaining about what happened to them in Nazi Germany."[16] A full 29 percent of all Americans polled agreed with the caricaturization of Jews as money-grubbing, and over "One-quarter of any group of people must be viewed as substantial, when it involves prejudice."[17]

Clearly, organized hate groups have a large base of potential supporters to draw from, and it is often personality clashes, disagreement regarding specific events, fear of alienation from co-workers, friends, or family, and fear of law enforcement that keep many people from joining organized hate groups, rather than basic disagreements in belief and ideology. Given that the basic beliefs embraced by organized hate groups are widespread, in addition to the fact that most hate-inspired violence is not committed by members of organized hate groups, we can conclude that narrow attention to organized hate groups is insufficient. They are clearly simply one manifestation of a more widespread problem. Focusing on only one small segment of the continuum, and treating it as an isolated, exceptional movement, distorts the problem, erases from view the rest of the continuum, and hinders our understanding of the organized hate movement itself. It must be seen within a continuum of racist, anti-Semitic, misogynist hate and fear. Fear certainly plays a key role, as we have observed in the current crises in both white and male identity. For those seeking to rearticulate and reaffirm disparaged identities, white supremacist discourse may seem attractive.

White supremacist discourse gains power precisely because it rearticulates mainstream racial and gender narratives once taken for granted. At the root of white supremacist racism is the assumption of essentialized racial and gender identities, usually assumed by the mainstream as well. These assumptions are easily manipulated by contemporary white supremacist discourse because they have such a long and powerful tradition, fully entrenched in white American "common sense." At a time when these assumptions are increasingly under attack, many seek confirmation and solace in clinging to these once taken for granted Truths.

Throughout this book I have attempted to deconstruct essentialized race and gender identities in white supremacist discourse. While it is imperative that we not uncritically reproduce the assumption of essentialized racial and gender identities, what are the consequences of this deconstruction? What are we left with? Are we forced, as a number of contemporary racial theorists suggest, to abandon racial identities? In her conclusion to her edited volume *American Mixed Race: The Culture of Microdiversity*, Naomi Zack contends that the best alternative to the reproduction of racial identities that perpetuate racist practice is to move beyond racial identities: "a more direct, and less semantically compromised, route to freedom would be to simply let the whole idea of 'race' go."[18]

Similarly, in *The Racialization of America*, Yehudi O. Webster deconstructs attempts to root racial identity in nature or biology, highlighting the arbitrariness of such designations. He asserts that because race has no basis in reality and is ambiguous, it must be abandoned: "an effective approach to black socioeconomic rehabilitation would be an abandoning of racial classification. Black liberation demands the negation of blackness."[19] Webster demands an abandonment of racial identities, proposing instead that we adopt an identity based on common humanity. I find this argument troublesome, however. While Webster criticizes social scientists' reliance on a supposed transparent reality from which they themselves are detached observers, he argues for the abandonment of racial categories because they do not correspond with reality and proposes instead a turn toward a common and essentialized human community whose reality remains unquestioned. Rather than asserting the social construction of identities, including race, ethnicity, nationality, sexuality, gender, and humanity, he contends that race and ethnicity are false identities.

If reality is socially constructed, there are no grounds from which to argue for the truth of some identities and the falsity of others, as the white supremacist project does. Rather, we can explore the construction of all identities. We can argue that some forms of identity ought to be retained, while others abandoned; however, not on the grounds that some are more real than others. Instead, our arguments to retain certain identities must be recognized as political decisions, based on strategic and ethical grounds. Webster posits the existence of a prediscursive human identity, yet as my research demonstrates, the realm of the human is constructed here *through* the production of racialized, gendered subjects. Individuals are not culturally intelligible humans prior to their racialization, as Webster maintains. Those improperly raced and gendered often do not qualify as human. The category of human, a socially constructed classification, does not have a stable existence outside of other constructed categories of identity.

Webster asserts that we ought to abandon race because it is a constructed category and because the construction of racial categories has been inextricably linked to racist practice. Should we also, then, abandon gender identities? Sexual identities? Ethnic identities? National identities? We can make the same arguments for many other socially constructed identities. Deconstruction, however, is not destructive; it does not entail the erasure of identity. To reveal racial categories as constructions is not to do away with them or to define them as false. It is, instead, as Judith Butler suggests,

> to free them from its metaphysical lodgings in order to understand what political interests were secured in and by that metaphysical placing, and thereby to permit the term to occupy and to serve very different political aims. To problematize the matter of bodies may entail an initial loss of epistemological certainty, but a loss of certainty is not the same as political nihilism.[20]

The deconstruction of essentialized race and gender identities is not the same thing as saying we need to abandon these categories of identity. Deconstruction is frequently misrepresented as a form of nihilism. This assumption, however, is rooted in the very same logic we saw evident throughout white supremacist discourse. Both assume that the questioning of difference necessarily means the erasure of difference. It is important to recognize that deconstruction can only be construed as nihilistic from within this binary framework, the assumption of which also must be deconstructed. This is the framework examined throughout this book as it structures white supremacist discourse, defining difference as requiring hierarchy and equality as resulting in sameness. As Michael Eric Dyson argues, "the goal should not be to transcend race, but to transcend the biased meanings associated with race. Ironically, the very attempt to transcend race by denying its presence reinforces its power to influence perceptions because it gains strength in secrecy."[21]

Affirmative action can serve as an example of the problem with these attempts to "move beyond" race. The colorblind policies favored by neoconservatives purport that race-based policies end up discriminating against white males. Gallagher's interviews with white students revealed that "much of the anger white students expressed stems from their belief that in a 'colorblind' society . . . race-based organizations are racist and 'discriminatory' toward whites. . . . The majority of white students believe affirmative action is unfair today because issues of overt racism, discrimination, and equal opportunity were addressed by their parents' generation in the 1960s."[22] These arguments for colorblind policy assume that racism is a thing of the past.

When race continues to shape the life experiences of all Americans, and when racial stratification is still deeply ingrained in our institutions and cultural practices, calls to move beyond race in our policies are simply racist. As Williams points out, "much is overlooked in the move to undo that which clearly and unfortunately matters just by labeling it that which 'makes no difference.' " Williams refers to this as the " 'I think therefore it is' school of idealism. 'I don't think about color, therefore your problems don't exist.' If only it were that easy."[23] In the current context we cannot abandon race-based policies.

Identity needs to be thought of differently, and this is the task that confronts us. Feminists have struggled for equality for women without having to demonstrate that women are identical to men. Traditionally, in order to argue for equality, women had to be shown to be the same as men; men set the standard. The supposedly neutral standard implicit in the law, medicine, sociology, and most institutions is androcentric. Women failed to fit this model based on male experience.

Lise Vogel demonstrates this dilemma clearly in her analysis of maternity policy in the workplace. Because only women experience pregnancy, they could not be fit into the "male as norm" model. Recognizing the futility of trying to meet this male standard, as well as the inherent dangers that accompany any arguments based on women's difference from men, feminists are theorizing ways of comprehending equality outside of a difference/equality framework.[24]

Rather than requiring the abandonment of racial and gender identity, which would be to fall into the trap of continuing this same difference/equality binary logic we have been interrogating, Ernesto Laclau suggests that deconstruction attempts "to trace the genealogy of the present dissolve the apparent obviousness of certain categories that are the trivialized and hardened sedimentations of tradition."[25] Rather than abandoning identity categories, their ontological status is questioned, and the power relations at stake in the production of those identities are exposed. Once we deconstruct these binary oppositions that construct identity, the possibilities of difference are opened up and proliferated, rather than annihilated.

While postmodernism is often wrongly dismissed as nonpolitical, it is quite the opposite; it makes political decisions *possible*. As Laclau further observes,

> if an ultimate ground is posited, political argument would consist in *discovering* the action of a reality external to the argument itself. If, however, there is no ultimate ground, political argument increases in importance because, through the conviction that it can contribute, it itself *constructs*, to a certain extent, the social reality.[26]

In other words, if ultimate foundations are posited, there is no space to make political decisions; the answers are always provided by those grounds. If those grounds are shown to be constructed, however, the space for making political decisions is opened up; indeed, every decision is political, and responsibility must be accepted. As Butler contends,

> the category of women does not become useless through deconstruction, but becomes one whose uses are no longer reified as "referents," and which stand a chance of being opened up, indeed, of coming to signify in ways that none of us can predict in advance. Surely, it must

be possible both to use the term, to use it tactically even as one is, as it were, used and positioned by it, and also to subject the term to a critique which interrogates the exclusionary operations and differential power-relations.[27]

In terms of my study of race and gender in white supremacist discourse, the deconstruction of racial and gender difference reveals their construction to be a political act, shaped by relations of power. The white supremacist assertion of essential race and gender identities posits race and gender as existing outside of their own discourse. They thus absolve themselves of any responsibility, so that white supremacist discourse describes itself as merely recognizing the "truth" of race and gender, which they claim others ignore. This is why they can depict themselves as benevolent, as in the articles discussed in chapter five, where it is declared that equality is a great myth and hoax, and that "I love my dog . . . but I'm not about to recognize her as my equal."[28] By constructing race and gender as natural and prediscursive differences, racial and gender hierarchies are reified and rationalized, and white supremacy justified. White supremacists absolve themselves of any responsibility for making political or ethical decisions. They present themselves as merely recognizing reality and claim that their only political/ethical choice is to choose to recognize that reality which others ignore.

Deconstructing racial and gender difference, however, allows us to see the white supremacist construction of race and gender as a political act, concerned with rationalizing white male privilege. Deconstructing race and gender opens up space for political argument against the white supremacist project. Attempts to combat the white supremacist movement by dismissing it as a deviant "lunatic fringe" have not been successful enough. We must engage the construction of essentialized race and gender identities within both mainstream and white supremacist discourse.

Rather than being the "antithesis of modern civilization,"[29] white supremacist discourse seeks to protect the same essential race and gender identities we all embrace. White supremacist discourse draws upon the very same tenets of modern, Enlightenment discourse that define race and gender as rooted in biology and genetics.

This book, then, highlights the relationship between race and racism. My argument is at odds with the distinction between racialism and racism advanced by Kwame Anthony Appiah in *In My Father's House: Africa in the Philosophy of Culture*. Appiah argues that the doctrine of racialism asserts that

there are heritable characteristics, possessed by members of our species, which allow us to divide them into a small set of races, in such a
way that all the members of these races share certain traits and tendencies. . . . These traits and tendencies characteristic of a race constitute, on the racialist view, a sort of racial essence.[30]

Appiah states that this heritable racial essence entails not only visible physical differences but moral and intellectual ability as well. "Racialism is not,
in itself, a doctrine that must be dangerous" he argues, "provided positive
moral qualities are distributed across the races, each can be respected, can
have its 'separate but equal' place."[31] While racism presupposes racialism,
Appiah argues that racialism does not require racism. The research presented throughout this book, however, challenges this distinction. The entire thrust of the white supremacist project is to maintain the boundaries
between constructed races. Because they construct a set number of races,
and believe each race to possess a unique, heritable, essence, their next step
is the maintenance of that essence. The focus of white supremacist anger is
aimed at threats to separation and, it follows, threats to the racial essence.
White supremacist publications often advance the same basic argument as
Appiah, asserting that there is nothing racist about wanting to maintain one's
race. In fact, white supremacists have adopted this very language, claiming
that they hate no one, they simply love their own race and want to secure
its existence.

I think it is a mistake, in this context in particular, to distinguish concep-
tually between racialism and racism and to believe they can be discon-
nected. It is inherently dangerous to construct racial categories believed
to signify heritable differences in character and ability. Their construction
necessarily involves border maintenance. This is a short step from the white
supremacist obsession with interracial sexuality; when these categories are
believed to be threatened, they will be defended, as we have witnessed.
What about those who exist astride the borders? We have seen the way
mixed-race people are treated in white supremacist discourse, and a growing literature by and about mixed-race people has challenged and decried
similar mainstream efforts at identity gatekeeping.[32]

The construction of race is central to racism. Contemporary political
struggles highlight this connection and, rather than respond by embracing
essentialist identities, attempt to subvert these classifications. For example,
in Oregon, citizens organizing against amendments that would make dis-

crimination against homosexuals legal, encouraged, as one response, that all concerned persons wear and display pink triangles. Citizens attempting to protest Ku Klux Klan violence adopted a similar approach in Billings, Montana. When Klan members vandalized homes that had menorahs displayed in their windows during Chanukah, the local newspaper printed pictures of menorahs for everyone in the town to display in their windows.[33] In both of these cases, rather than organizing against oppressive actions by embracing essential racial and sexual identities, the political responses instead subvert the construction of the essential identities at the heart of these racist acts and discriminatory laws, in contrast to traditional approaches that admit "the natural existence of 'races' even while opposing social distinctions among them."[34]

Emphasizing attention to the centrality of conceptions of race to racism, this book reads white supremacist discourse not as a discourse about race, but as the production of race. Studies of the white supremacist movement that uncritically take race for granted are a part of the problem, reifying notions of essential racial identity, the very project of the white supremacist movement.

White supremacist discourse rearticulates dominant discourses on race and gender; therefore, any effective political response to the white supremacist movement must also attack these mainstream narratives. This does not necessarily mean negating racial and gender identities, but revealing their constructedness and continually deconstructing their foundations. We cannot abandon identities simply because they are revealed to be constructions, for all identities are constructions. We have no choice but to live within our constructions—we cannot live without them. But any construction can be reconstructed. As Benedict Anderson asserts, "all communities larger than primordial villages of face-to-face contact (and perhaps even these) are imagined. Communities are to be distinguished not by their falsity/genuineness, but by the style in which they are imagined."[35]

It has been my goal to highlight the danger of taking foundational categories of race and gender for granted in white supremacist, mainstream, and even social science discourse. Like white supremacists, sociologists have long taken race and gender identity as given starting points, failing to explore their own complicity in the rearticulation and reification of these categories. While this book explores white supremacist discourse, it also emphasizes the necessity of interrogating the positions from which we write. We need to question our own, and our discipline's, assumptions about race and gender, implicit in our research approach from the start, and explore our own discourses as sites of the construction of race and gender. I suggest that our own discourses too often partake in the central project of white supremacy: the construction and maintenance of essential racial and gender differences. It is easy to condemn racism. It is much more difficult to interrogate our own.

NOTES

1. *The National Alliance Bulletin* June 1980, 4.
2. Lipsitz 1995.
3. hooks 1990, 54.
4. hooks 1990, 54.
5. Williams 1997, 4.
6. Frankenberg 1993; Gallagher 1995; Ignatiev and Garvey 1996; Lucal 1996; McIntosh 1992; Williams 1997.
7. Gallagher 1995, 176–77.
8. Ignatiev and Garvey 1996, 10.
9. Williams 1997.
10. George and Wilcox 1992, 54.
11. Dyson 1993, 144–45.
12. Sheffield 1992, 389.
13. Sheffield 1992, 391.
14. Anti-Defamation League 1995, 96.
15. Coates 1987, 197.
16. Coates 1987, 198.
17. Coates 1987, 199.
18. Zack 1995, 307.
19. Webster 1992, 193.
20. Butler 1993a, 30.
21. Dyson 1993.
22. Gallagher 1995, 175.
23. Williams 1997, 4.
24. Scott 1988a; Tavris 1992; Vogel 1993.
25. Laclau 1988, 65.
26. Laclau 1988, 79.
27. Butler 1993a, 29.

28. *White Power* March 1973, 6.
29. Bauman 1989, 7.
30. Appiah 1992, 13.
31. Appiah 1992, 12.
32. Anzaldua 1987; Zack 1993; Zack 1995.
33. These events were the subject of the PBS documentary *Not In Our Town*, 1996.
34. Ignatiev and Garvey 1996, 10.
35. Anderson 1983, 6.

BIBLIOGRAPHY

Adams, Romanzo. 1937. *Interracial marriage in Hawaii*. New York: Macmillan.

Agger, Ben. 1994. Derrida for sociology? A comment on Fuchs and Ward. *American Sociological Review* 59(August):501–5.

Aho, James A. 1990. *The politics of righteousness: Idaho Christian patriotism*. Seattle: University of Washington Press.

———. 1994. *This thing of darkness: A sociology of the enemy*. Seattle: University of Washington Press.

Allen, Theodore. 1994. *The invention of the white race*. New York: Verso.

Andersen, Margaret, and Patricia Hill Collins. 1992. *Race, class, and gender: An anthology*. Belmont, Calif.: Wadsworth.

Anderson, Benedict. 1983. *Imagined communities*. London: Verso.

Andolsen, Barbara Hilkert. 1986. *Daughters of Jefferson, daughters of bootblacks*. Macon, Ga.: Mercer University Press.

The Anti-Defamation League of B'nai B'rith. 1988a. *Extremism on the right: A handbook*. New York.

———. 1988b. *Hate groups in America: A record of bigotry and violence*. New York.

———. 1991. *The KKK today: A 1991 status report*. New York.

———. 1995. *The Skinhead international: A worldwide survey of neo-Nazi Skinheads*. New York.

———. 1996a. *Danger: Extremism, the major vehicles and voices on America's far-right fringe*. New York.

———. 1996b. *The web of hate: Extremists exploit the Internet*. New York.

Anzaldua, Gloria. 1987. *Borderlands la frontera*. San Francisco: Aunt Lute Books.

Appiah, Kwame Anthony. 1992. *In my father's house: Africa in the philosophy of culture*. New York: Oxford.

Arnett, Elsa C., and Tony Pugh. 1997. Mixed-race unions up. *Denver Post*, 6 December.

Baker, Houston A. 1993. Scene . . . not heard. In *Reading Rodney King/ reading urban uprising*, edited by Robert Gooding-Williams. New York: Routledge.

Balibar, Etienne, and Immanuel Wallerstein. 1991. *Race, nation, class: Ambiguous identities*. London: Verso.

Banton, Michael, and Jonathan Harwood. 1975. *The race concept*. New York: Praeger.

Barkun, Michael. 1994. *Religion and the racist right: The origins of the Christian Identity movement*. Chapel Hill: University of North Carolina Press.

Barron, Milton L. 1972. Intergroup aspects of choosing a mate. In *The blending American*, edited by Milton L. Barron. Chicago: Quadrangle Books.

Bauman, Zygmunt. 1989. *Modernity and the holocaust*. Ithaca, N.Y.: Cornell University Press.

Bell, Daniel, ed. 1964. *The radical right*. Garden City, N.Y.: Anchor Books.

Berger, Peter L., and Thomas Luckmann. 1966. *The social construction of reality: A treatise in the sociology of knowledge*. Garden City, N.Y.: Anchor Books.

Berlet, Chip, ed. 1995. *Eyes right: Challenging the right wing backlash*. Boston: South End Press.

Bhaba, Homi K. 1990. Interrogating identity: The postcolonial prerogative. In *Anatomy of racism*, edited by David Theo Goldberg. Minneapolis: University of Minnesota Press.

Blau, Peter M., Terry C. Blum, and Joseph E. Schwartz. 1987. Heterogeneity and intermarriage. *American Sociological Review* 47(February):45–62.

Blee, Kathleen. 1991a. Women in the 1920s' Ku Klux Klan movement. *Feminist Studies* 1(Spring):57–77.

———. 1991b. *Women of the Klan: Racism and gender in the 1920s*. Berkeley: University of California Press.

———. 1995. Engendering conspiracy: Women in rightist theories and movements. Paper presented at the Northwest Coalition Against Malicious Harassment 1995 symposium, 13 October, in Portland, Oreg.

———. 1996. Becoming a racist: Women in contemporary Ku Klux Klan and neo-Nazi groups. *Gender and Society* 10, no. 6(December):680–702.

Blum, Terry C. 1984. Racial inequality and salience: An examination of Blau's theory of social structure. *Social Forces* 62, no. 3(March):607–17.

Bogardus, Emory S. 1968. Comparing racial distance in Ethiopia, South Africa and the United States. *Sociology and Social Research* 52(January):149–56.

Brewer, Rose M. 1989. Black women and feminist sociology: The emerging perspective. *The American Sociologist* 20, no. 1:57–70.

Butler, Judith. 1990. *Gender trouble: Feminism and the subversion of identity.* New York: Routledge.

———. 1991. Imitation and gender insubordination. In *Inside/out: Lesbian theories, gay theories,* edited by Diana Fuss. London: Routledge.

———. 1993a. *Bodies that matter: On the discursive limits of sex.* New York: Routledge.

———. 1993b. Endangered/endangering: Schematic racism and white paranoia. In *Reading Rodney King/reading urban uprising,* edited by Robert Gooding-Williams. New York: Routledge.

Carby, Hazel. 1986. "On the threshold of woman's era": Lynching, empire, and sexuality in black feminist theory. In *"Race," writing and difference,* edited by Henry Louis Gates Jr. Chicago: University of Chicago Press.

———. 1990. The politics of difference. *Ms.* (September/October):85.

———. 1992. The multicultural wars. *Radical History Review* 54(Fall):7–18.

Cazares, Ralph B., Edward Murguia, and W. Parker Frisbie. 1984. Mexican American intermarriage in a nonmetropolitan context. *Social Science Quarterly* 65:626–34.

Centers, Richard. 1949. Marital selection and occupational strata. *American Journal of Sociology* 54:508–19.

Cerroni-Long, E. L. 1984. Marrying out: Sociocultural and psychological implications of intermarriage. *Journal of Comparative Family Studies* 16, no. 1:25–46.

Chalmers, David M. 1987. *Hooded Americanism: The first century of the history of the Ku Klux Klan.* Durham: Duke University Press.

Clatterbaugh, Ken. 1995. Mythopoetic foundations and new age patriarchy. In *The politics of manhood: Profeminist men respond to the mythopoetic men's movement (and the mythopoetic leaders answer),* edited by Michael S. Kimmel. Philadelphia: Temple University Press.

Coates, James. 1987. *Armed and dangerous: The rise of the survivalist right.* New York: Hill and Wang.

Collins, Margaret S., Irving W. Wainer, and Theodore A. Bremner. 1981. *Science and the question of human equality*. Boulder: Westview Press.

Collins, Patricia Hill. 1990. *Black feminist thought: Knowledge, consciousness, and the politics of empowerment*. Boston: Unwin Hyman.

Conason, Joe, Alfred Ross, and Lee Cokorinos. 1996. The Promise Keepers are coming: The third wave of the religious right. *The Nation*, 7 October, 11–19.

Cope, Edward D. 1890. Two perils of the Indo-European. *Open Court*, III, 48(January 23), 2054.

Cornell, Drucilla L. 1992. Gender, sex, and equivalent rights. In *Feminists theorize the political*, edited by Judith Butler and Joan Scott. New York: Routledge.

Crawford, Robert, and Devin Burghart. 1997. Guns and gavels: Common law courts, militias and white supremacy. In *The second revolution: States rights, sovereignty, and power of the county*, edited by Eric Ward. Seattle: Peanut Butter Publishing.

Crenshaw, Kimberlè, and Gary Peller. 1993. Reel time/real justice. In *Reading Rodney King/reading urban uprising*, edited by Robert Gooding-Williams. New York: Routledge.

Crosby, Christina. 1992. Dealing with differences. In *Feminists theorize the political*, edited by Judith Butler and Joan Scott. New York: Routledge.

Culler, Jonathan. 1982. *On deconstruction: Theory and criticism after structuralism*. Ithaca, N.Y.: Cornell University Press.

Daniels, Jessie. 1997. *White lies: Race, class, gender, and sexuality in white supremacist discourse*. New York: Routledge.

Davis, Angela. 1983. *Women, race and class*. New York: Vintage Books.

Davis, F. James. 1991. *Who is black? One nation's definition*. University Park: Pennsylvania State University Press.

———. 1995. The Hawaiian alternative to the one-drop rule. In *American mixed race: The culture of microdiversity*, edited by Naomi Zack. Lanham, Md.: Rowman & Littlefield.

Davis, Kingsley. 1941. Intermarriage in caste societies. *American Anthropologist* 43(July–September):376–95.

Dees, Morris, with James Corcoran. 1996. *Gathering storm: America's militia threat*. New York: Harper Perennial.

Derrida, Jacques. 1974. Of grammatology. Translated by Gayatri Chakravorty Spivak. Baltimore: Johns Hopkins University Press.

———. 1982. *Margins of philosophy*. Translated by Alan Bass. Chicago: University of Chicago Press.

Diamond, Sara. 1995. *Roads to dominion: Right-wing movements and political power in the United States*. New York: Guilford Press.

Dixon, Thomas. 1902. *The leopard's spots: A romance of the white man's burden—1865–1900*. New York: Doubleday, Page, and Co.

Donovan, Josephine. 1994. *Feminist theory: The intellectual traditions of American feminism*. New York: Continuum.

Dowd Hall, Jacquelyn. 1992. "The mind that burns in each body": Women, rape, and racial violence. In *Race, class, and gender: An anthology*, edited by Margaret L. Andersen and Patricia Hill Collins. Belmont, Calif.: Wadsworth.

Doyle, Laura. 1994. *Bordering on the body: The racial matrix of modern fiction and culture*. Oxford: Oxford University Press.

Dyson, Michael Eric. 1993. *Reflecting black: African American cultural criticism*. Minneapolis: University of Minnesota Press.

Eagleton, Terry. 1983. *Literary theory: An introduction*. Minneapolis: University of Minnesota Press.

Elkhart Truth. 1992. Couple shot because of assailant's beliefs. December 20.

Epstein, Cynthia Fuchs. 1988. *Deceptive distinctions: Sex, gender, and the social order*. New York: The Russell Sage Foundation.

Ezekiel, Raphael S. 1995. *The racist mind: Portraits of American neo-Nazis and Klansmen*. New York: Viking.

Fabian, Johannes. 1983. *Time and the other: How anthropology makes its object*. New York: Columbia University Press.

Faludi, Susan. 1991. *Backlash: The undeclared war against American women*. New York: Crown.

Feagin, Joe, and Hernan Vera. 1995. *White racism*. New York: Routledge.

Ferber, Abby L. 1992. The "far right": Constructing boundaries. Paper presented at the Fascism(s): Roots/Extensions/Replays Conference, April, at The University of Oregon, Eugene, Oregon.

———. 1994. Regulating interracial sexuality: The production of racialized, gendered subjects in contemporary white supremacist discourse, Ph.D. diss., University of Oregon.

———. 1995a. Exploring the social construction of race: Social science research and the study of interracial relationships. In *American mixed race:*

The culture of microdiversity. edited by Naomi Zack. Lanham, Md.: Rowman & Littlefield.

————. 1995b. "Shame of white men": Interracial sexuality and the construction of white masculinity in contemporary white supremacist discourse. *Masculinities*, 3, no. 2 (Summer):1–24.

————. 1996. Analyzing the gendered politics of right-wing racial movements. *Conspiracies: Real grievances, paranoia, and mass movements,* edited by Eric Ward. Seattle: Peanut Butter Publishing.

————. 1997. Of Mongrels and Jews: The deconstruction of racialised identities in white supremacist discourse. *Social Identities* 3, no. 2 (April):193–208.

————. 1998a. Deconstructing whiteness: The intersections of race and gender in U.S. white supremacist discourse. *Ethnic and Racial Studies* 21, no. 1 (January):48–63.

————. 1998b. "White supremacist movement in the U.S. today," in *Race and Ethnic Conflict*, edited by Fred L. Pincus and Howard J. Ehrlich, second edition. Boulder, Colo.: Westview.

Fishkin, Shelley Fisher. 1995. Interrogating "whiteness," complicating "blackness": Remapping American culture. *American Quarterly* 47, no. 3 (September):428–66.

Flax, Jane. 1993. Multiples: On the contemporary politics of subjectivity. *Human Studies* 16, nos.1–2:33–49.

Flintoff, Anne. 1993. One of the boys? Gender identities in physical education initial teacher education. In *'Race,' gender and the education of teachers*, edited by Iram Siraj-Blatchford. Philadelphia: Open University Press.

Flynn, Kevin, and Gary Gerhardt. 1989. *The silent brotherhood: Inside America's racist underground.* New York: Free Press.

Foucault, Michel. 1972. *Power/knowledge: Selected interviews and other writings 1972–1977*, edited by Colin Gordon. New York: Pantheon.

————. 1978. *The history of sexuality: An introduction.* New York: Vintage.

Fraiman, Susan. 1994. Geometries of race and gender: Eve Sedgewick, Spike Lee, Charlayne Hunter-Gault. *Feminist Studies* 20(Spring):67–84.

Frankenberg, Ruth. 1993. *White women, race matters: The social construction of whiteness.* Minneapolis: University of Minnesota Press.

Fraser, Steven. 1995. *The bell curve wars: Race, intelligence, and the future of America.* New York: Basic Books.

Frazier, E. Franklin. 1957. *The Negro in the United States*. New York: Macmillan.

Fuss, Diana. 1989. *Essentially speaking: Feminism, nature and difference*. New York: Routledge.

————, ed. 1991. *Inside/out: Lesbian theories, gay theories*. London: Routledge.

Gallagher, Charles. 1995. White reconstruction in the university. *Socialist Review* 24, no. 1 & 2:165–87.

Game, Ann. 1991. *Undoing the social: Towards a deconstructive sociology*. Toronto: University of Toronto Press.

Garcia, Alma M. 1990. The development of Chicana feminist discourse, 1970–1980. In *Unequal sisters*, edited by Ellen Carol Dubois and Vicki Ruize. New York: Routledge.

Garfinkel, Harold. 1967. *Studies in ethnomethodology*. New York: Polity Press.

Gates, Henry Louis, Jr., and Cornel West. 1996. *The future of the race*. New York: Vintage.

George, John, and Laird Wilcox. 1992. *Nazis, Communists, Klansmen, and others on the fringe*. Buffalo, N.Y.: Prometheus.

Giddings, Paula. 1984. *When and where I enter: The impact of black women on race and sex in America*. New York: William Morrow.

Gilmore, Ruth Wilson. 1993. Terror austerity race gender excess theater. In *Reading Rodney King/reading urban uprising*, edited by Robert Gooding-Williams. New York: Routledge.

Goldberg, David Theo. 1990. *Anatomy of racism*. Minneapolis: University of Minnesota Press.

————. 1993. *Racist culture: Philosophy and the politics of meaning*. Oxford: Blackwell.

Gooding-Williams, Robert. 1993. *Reading Rodney King/reading urban uprising*. New York: Routledge.

Gordon, Milton M. 1964. *Assimilation in American life*. New York: Oxford.

Gould, Stephen Jay. 1981. *The mismeasure of man*. New York: Norton.

Gurak, Douglas T., and Joseph P. Fitzpatrick. 1982. Intermarriage among hispanic ethnic groups in New York City. *American Journal of Sociology* 87, no. 4:921–34.

Hall, Stuart. 1982. The rediscovery of "ideology": Return of the repressed in media studies. In *Culture, media and society*, edited by Michael Gurevitch. London: Methuen.

————. 1990. Cultural identity and diaspora. In *Identity: Community, cultural, difference*, edited by Jonathan Rutherford. London: Lawrence and Wishart.

Harding, Sandra. 1986. *The science question in feminism*. Ithaca, N.Y.: Cornell University Press.

Harper, Suzanne. 1993. The brotherhood: Race and gender ideologies in the white supremacist movement. Ph.D. diss., University of Texas, Austin.

————. 1994. Subordinating masculinities/racializing masculinities: Representations of white, black and Jewish men in white supremacist publications. Paper presented at the North Central Sociological Association's Annual Meeting, April, Columbus, Ohio.

Heath, Stephen. 1982. *The sexual fix*. London: Macmillan.

Hekman, Susan J. 1990. *Gender and knowledge: Elements of a postmodern feminism*. Boston: Northeastern University Press.

Hernton, Calvin C. 1965. *Sex and racism in America*. New York: Grove.

Hernstein, Richard J., and Charles Murray. 1994. *The bell curve: Intelligence and class structure in American life*. New York: Free Press.

Higginbotham, Evelyn Brooks. 1992. African American women's history and the metalanguage of race. *Signs: Journal of Women in Culture and Society* 17, no. 2:251–74.

Hollingshead, August B. 1950. Cultural factors in the selection of marriage mates. *American Sociological Review* 15:619–27.

hooks, bell. 1981. *Ain't I a woman? Black women and feminism*. Boston: South End Press.

————. 1984. *Feminist theory from margin to center*. Boston: South End Press.

————. 1990. *Yearning: Race, gender, and cultural politics*. Boston: South End Press.

————. 1994. *Outlaw culture: Resisting representations*. New York: Routledge.

Hubbard, Ruth. 1992. *The politics of women's biology*. New Brunswick, N.J.: Rutgers University Press.

Hughes, Henry. 1854. *Treatise on sociology, theoretical and practical*. Philadelphia: Lippincott, Grambo 7 Co.

Hunt, Darnell. 1996. Playing the "race card" in "colorblind" times: Raced ways of seeing, "evidence," and the "trial of the century." Paper presented at the American Sociological Association's Annual Meeting, August, New York City.

Ignatiev, Noel, and John Garvey. 1996. *Race traitor*. New York: Routledge.

Ilter, Tugrul. 1994. The unassimilable otherness of the "post" of postmodern and the radicality of radical sociology. *Critical Sociology* 20 no. 2:51–80.

Intelligence Project of the Southern Poverty Law Center. 1998. *Intelligence report*. Issue 89, Winter.

Jenness, Valerie, and Kendal Broad. 1997. *Hate crimes: New social movements and the politics of violence*. New York: Aldine De Gruyter.

Jones, Jacqueline. 1985. *Labor of love, labor of sorrow: Black women, work, and the family from slavery to the present*. New York: Basic Books.

Jordan, Winthrop. 1969. *White over black*. Chapel Hill: University of North Carolina Press.

Katz, William Loren. 1987. *The invisible empire: The Ku Klux Klan impact on history*. Seattle: Open Hand Publishing.

Kavanagh, James H. 1990. Ideology. In *Critical terms for literary study*, edited by Frank Lentriccia and Thomas McLaughlin. Chicago: University of Chicago Press.

Kearl, Michael C., and Edward Murguia. 1985. Age differences of spouses in Mexican American intermarriage: Exploring the cost of minority assimilation. *Social Science Quarterly* 66:453–60.

Keith, Vera M., and Cedric Herring. 1991. Skin tone and stratification in the black community. *American Journal of Sociology* 97, no. 3:760–78.

Kennedy, Ruby J. 1944. Single or triple melting pot? *American Journal of Sociology* 39:331–39.

Kimmel, Michael S., 1987. The contemporary "crisis" of masculinity in historical perspective. In *The Making of Masculinities: The New Men's Studies*, edited by Harry Brod. Boston: Allen and Unwin.

———. 1994. Masculinity as homophobia: Fear, shame, and silence in the construction of gender identity. In *Theorizing Masculinities*, edited by Harry Brod and Michael Kaufman. Thousand Oaks, Calif.: Sage.

Kintz, Linda. 1993. Sacred representations: Spiritual gender and the religious right. Paper presented at the *Soundings Conference*, at the University of Oregon, Eugene.

Kitano, Harry H. L., and Lynn Kyung Chai. 1982. Korean interracial marriage. *Marriage and Family Review* 5, no. 1:75–81.

Kitano, Harry H. L., and Wai-tsang Yeung. 1982. Chinese interracial marriage. *Marriage and Family Review* 5, no. 1: 35–48.

Klanwatch. 1991. Knights of the Ku Klux Klan: The "new" face of racism. In *Klanwatch Intelligence Report*. Montgomery, Ala.: The Klanwatch Project of the Southern Poverty Law Center.

———. 1992. *Annual report*. Montgomery, Ala.: The Klanwatch Project of the Southern Poverty Law Center.

———. 1993. The Midwest's top neo-nazi: Gerhard Lauck and the NSDAP-AO. In *Klanwatch Intelligence Report*. Montgomery, Ala.: The Klanwatch Project of the Southern Poverty Law Center. 66(April):8–9.

Laclau, Ernesto. 1988. Politics and the limits of modernity. In *Universal abandon? The politics of postmodernism*, edited by Andrew Ross. Minneapolis: University of Minnesota Press.

Langer, Elinor. 1990. The American neo-Nazi movement today. *The Nation* 16, no. 23 (July):82–107.

Laqueur, Thomas. 1990. *Making sex: Body and gender from the Greeks to Freud*. Cambridge: Harvard University Press.

Lipset, Seymour Martin, and Earl Raab. 1970. *Politics of unreason: Right-wing extremism in America, 1790–1970*. New York: Harper & Row.

Lipsitz, George. 1995. The possessive investment in whiteness: Racialized social democracy and the "white" problem in American studies. *American Quarterly* 47, no.3 (September):369–87.

Lorde, Audre. 1984. *Sister outsider*. Trumansburg, Pa.: Crossing Press.

Lott, Eric. 1993. *Love and theft: Blackface minstrelsy and the American working class*. Oxford: Oxford University Press.

Lucal, Betsy. 1996. Oppression *and* privilege: Toward a relational conceptualization of race. *Teaching Sociology* 24 (July):245–55.

Macdonald, Andrew [pseudonym of William Pierce]. 1978. *The Turner diaries*. Hillsboro, Va.: National Vanguard Books.

Maclean, Nancy. 1994. *Behind the mask of chivalry: The making of the second Ku Klux Klan*. New York: Oxford.

Marger, Martin N. 1994. *Race and ethnic relations: American and global perspectives*. Belmont, Calif.: Wadsworth.

Marks, Jonathan. 1994. Black, White, Other. *Natural History* (December):32–35.

Marks, Kathy. 1996. *Faces of right-wing extremism*. Boston: Branden.

McIntosh, Peggy. 1992. White privilege and male privilege: A personal account of coming to see correspondences through work in women's studies. *Race, class and gender: An anthology*, edited by Margaret Andersen and Patricia Hill Collins. Belmont, Calif.: Wadsworth.

Mecklin, John Moffatt. 1924. *The Ku Klux Klan: A study of the American mind*. New York: Harcourt, Brace.

Mencke, John G. 1979. *Mulattoes and race mixture: American attitudes and images, 1865–1918*. Ann Arbor, Mich.: University Microfilms Research Press.

Merton, Robert K. 1941. Intermarriage and the social structure: Fact and theory. *Psychiatry* 4 (August):361–74.

Minh-ha, Trinh T. 1989. *Woman, native, other: Writing postcoloniality and feminism*. Bloomington: Indiana University Press.

Monahan, Thomas P. 1976a. The occupational class of couples entering into interracial marriages. *Journal of Comparative Family Studies* 7, no. 2:175–92.

———. 1976b. An overview of statistics on interracial marriage in the United States, with data on its extent from 1963–1970. *Journal of Marriage and the Family* (May):223–31.

———. 1979. Interracial marriage and divorce in Kansas and the question of instability of mixed marriages. In *Cross-cultural perspectives in mate selection*, edited by G. Kurian. Westport, Conn.: Greenwood Press.

Moore, Leonard J. 1991. *Citizen klansmen: The Ku Klux Klan in Indiana, 1921–1928*. Chapel Hill: University of North Carolina Press.

Moore, Zena. 1995. Check the box that best describes you. In *American mixed race: The culture of microdiversity*, edited by Naomi Zack. Lanham, Md.: Rowman & Littlefield.

Morrison, Toni. 1992. *Playing in the dark: Whiteness and the literary imagination*. New York: Vintage.

Murguia, Edward. 1982. *Chicano intermarriage: A theoretical and empirical study*. San Antonio, Tex.: Trinity University Press.

Murguia, Edward, and W. Parker Frisbie. 1977. Trends in Mexican American intermarriage: Recent findings in perspective. *Social Science Quarterly* 374:389.

Myrdal, Gunnar. 1944. *An American dilemma: The Negro problem and modern democracy*. New York: Harper and Brothers.

Nicholson, Linda. 1994. Interpreting gender. *Signs: Journal of Women in Culture and Society* 20(Autumn):79–105.

Novick, Michael. 1995. *White lies white power: The fight against white supremacy and reactionary violence*. Monroe, Maine: Common Courage Press.

Omi, Michael. 1991. Shifting the blame: Racial ideology and politics in the post-civil rights era. *Critical Sociology* 18, no.3(Fall):77–98.

Omi, Michael, and Howard Winant. 1986. *Racial formation in the United States: From the 1960s to the 1980s.* New York: Routledge.

Parkman, Margaret A., and Jack Sawyer. 1967. Dimensions of ethnic inter-marriage in Hawaii. *American Sociological Review* 32:593–608.

Ridgeway, James. 1990. *Blood in the face.* New York: Thunder's Mouth Press.

Riley, Denise. 1988. *"Am I that name?" Feminism and the category of "women" in history.* Minneapolis: University of Minnesota.

Roberts, Regina M. 1997. Assault on "cyberhate" launched. *Denver Post,* 30 November.

Roediger, David R. 1991. *The wages of whiteness: Race and the making of the American working class.* New York: Verso.

Russell, Kathy, Midge Wilson, and Ronald Hall. 1992. *The color complex: The politics of skin color among African Americans.* New York: Doubleday.

Sacks, Karen Brodkin. 1994. "How Did Jews Become White Folks?" In *Race,* edited by Steven Gregory and Roger Sanjek. New Brunswick, N.J.: Rutgers University Press.

Saxton, Alexander. 1987. *The rise and fall of the white republic.* New York: Routledge.

Schwartz, Howard, and Jerry Jacobs. 1979. *Qualitative sociology: A method to the madness.* New York: Free Press.

Schwertfeger, Margaret M. 1982. Interethnic marriage and divorce in Hawaii: A panel study of 1968 first marriages. *Marriage and Family Review* 5, no. 1:49–59.

Scott, Joan W. 1988a. Deconstructing equality-versus-difference: Or, the uses of poststructuralist theory for feminism. *Feminist Studies* 14, no.1 (Spring):33–50.

———. 1988b. *Gender and the politics of history.* New York: Columbia University Press.

Segrest, Mab. 1996. *Memoir of a race traitor.* Boston: South End Press.

Seidman, Steven. 1991. The end of sociological theory: The postmodern hope. *Sociological Theory* 9, no.2:134–36.

Shafer, Robert Jones. 1980. *A guide to historical method.* 3rd ed. Chicago: The Dorsey Press.

Shanklin, Eugenia. 1994. *Anthropology and race*. Belmont, Calif.: Wadsworth.

Sheffield, Carole. 1992. Hate violence. In *Race, class and gender in the U.S.: An integrated study*, edited by Paula Rothenberg. New York: St. Martin's.

Sims, Patsy. 1978. *The Klan*. New York: Stein and Day.

Smedley, Audrey. 1993. *Race in North America: Origin and evolution of a worldview*. Boulder, Colo.: Westview Press.

Smith, Dorothy E. 1987. *The everyday world as problematic: A feminist sociology*. Boston: Northeastern University Press.

Smith, Valerie. 1994. Split affinities: The case of interracial rape. In *Theorizing feminism: Parallel trends in the humanities and social sciences*, edited by Anne C. Herrmann and Abigail J. Stewart. Boulder, Colo.: Westview Press.

Sontag, Susan. 1978. *Illness as metaphor*. New York: Anchor.

Spelman, Elizabeth. 1988. *Inessential woman*. Boston: Beacon Press.

Spickard, Paul R. 1989. *Mixed blood: Intermarriage and ethnic identity in twentieth-century America*. Madison: University of Wisconsin Press.

Steinberg, Stephen. 1995. *Turning back: The retreat from racial justice in American thought and policy*. Boston: Beacon Press.

Stevens, Gillian. 1985. Nativity, intermarriage and mother-tongue shift. *American Sociological Review* 50 (February):74–83.

Strauss, Anselm. 1987. *Qualitative analysis for social scientists*. Cambridge: Cambridge University Press.

Tavris, Carol. 1992. *The mismeasure of woman*. New York: Touchstone.

Tompkins, Jane. 1992. *West of everything: The inner life of westerns*. New York: Oxford.

Vogel, Lise. 1993. *Mothers on the job: Maternity policy in the U.S. workplace*. New Brunswick, N.J.: Rutgers University Press.

Wade, Wyn Craig. 1987. *The fiery cross: The Ku Klux Klan in America*. New York: Simon and Schuster.

Wallace, Michele. 1990. *Invisibility blues: From pop to theory*. London: Verso.

Ward, Eric, ed. 1996. *Conspiracies: Real grievances, paranoia, and mass movements*. Seattle: Peanut Butter Publishing.

———, ed. 1997. *The second revolution: States rights, sovereignty, and power of the county*. Seattle: Peanut Butter Publishing.

Ware, Vron. 1992. *Beyond the pale: White women, racism and history*. London: Verso.

Webster, Yehudi O. 1992. *The racialization of America*. New York: St. Martin's.

Weedon, Chris. 1987. *Feminist practice and poststructuralist theory*. Cambridge: Blackwell.

Wells, Ida B. 1970. *Crusade For justice: The autobiography of Ida B. Wells*, edited by Alfreda M. Duster. Chicago: University of Chicago Press.

West, Cornel. 1982. *Prophesy deliverance! An Afro-American revolutionary Christianity*. Philadelphia: Westminster Press.

———. 1993. *Race matters*. Boston: Beacon Press.

Williams, Patricia J. 1997. *Seeing a color-blind future: The paradox of race*. New York: Noonday Press.

Williams, Richard. 1990. *Hierarchical structures and social value: The creation of black and Irish identities in the United States*. Cambridge: Cambridge University Press.

Williamson, Joel. 1980. *New people: Miscegenation and mulattoes in the United States*. New York: New York University Press.

Woods, Jim. 1994. Rhetoric of hate groups same, rights lawyer says. *Columbus Dispatch*, 6 March, 5D.

Young, Iris Marion. 1990. The ideal of community and the politics of difference. In *Feminism/Postmodernism*, edited by Linda J. Nicholson. New York: Routledge.

Young, Robert J. C. 1995. *Colonial desire: Hybridity in theory, culture and race*. New York: Routledge.

Zack, Naomi. 1993. *Race and mixed race*. Philadelphia: Temple University Press.

———. 1995. *American mixed race: The culture of microdiversity*. Lanham, Md.: Rowman & Littlefield.

Zatarain, Michael. 1990. *David Duke: Evolution of a Klansman*. Gretna, La.: Pelican Publishing.

Zeskind, Leonard. 1986. *The "Christian Identity" movement*. Atlanta: Center for Democratic Renewal, published by the Division of Church and Society of the National Council of the Churches of Christ in the U.S.A.

———. 1995. Armed and dangerous: The NRA, militias and white supremacists are fostering a network of right wing warriors. *Rolling Stone*, 2 November.

APPENDIX
PRIMARY SOURCES

PERIODICALS

The following periodicals were reviewed for the years listed. While I examined every issue for every year contained within the University of Oregon's Stimely collection, occasionally an issue number was missing. I have no way of knowing whether the collection was simply missing the issue or if the periodical missed an issue date, because publication of various periodicals is occasionally sporadic or inconsistent in terms of dates. Nevertheless, the majority of the issues printed for the years listed were contained within the collection and thus reviewed.

1. *Instauration* (1976–1983): "Seemingly intellectual," racist and anti-Semitic magazine published by Howard Allen Enterprises, in Cape Canaveral, Florida. Little is known about this corporation. Edited by Wilmot Robertson, pen name of the author of *The Dispossessed Majority*, *Instauration* has been advertised as "essentially a monthly update" of *The Dispossessed Majority*. *Instauration* is concerned with putting " 'Northern Europeans back on the evolutionary track' and with 'the consolidation, security and advancement of the Northern European peoples.' " John Tyndall, leader of Great Britain's neo-fascist National Front, has called *Instauration* "a highly articulate and stimulating monthly . . . enjoying growing popularity among . . . the National Front" (Anti-Defamation League 1988a, 152).

2. *The National Alliance Bulletin* (1978–1980) and

3. *National Vanguard* (1978–1984): both periodicals are published by the National Alliance, in Mill Point, West Virginia, a neo-Nazi racist group headed by William Pierce and founded in 1970. The National Alliance originated from the Youth for Wallace campaign in 1968, run by Willis A. Carto,

but split from Carto in 1970 and became the National Alliance, run by former members of George Lincoln Rockwell's American Nazi Party. William
Pierce had edited Rockwell's *National Socialist World,* and after Rockwell's
death in 1967, he became leader of the American Nazi Party, subsequently
renamed the National Socialist White People's Party, lead by Matt Koehl.
In 1984, Pierce established a 346-acre compound in West Virginia called
the Cosmotheist Community Church.

4. *The New Order* (1979–1983): published by Gerhard Lauck, in Lincoln, Nebraska. Lauck heads the neo-Nazi National Socialist German Workers Party (known overseas as NSDAP-AO). "The NSDAP-AO's circulation
is so widespread that it allegedly is recognized by the West German government as the primary source of propaganda materials to [their] underground"
(Klanwatch Intelligence Report 1993, 8). *The New Order* is widely read and
distributed by various white supremacist groups because "membership and
distribution materials are easy to obtain" (Klanwatch Intelligence Report
1993, 9). Still going strong, the NSDAP-AO has benefited from the recent
surge in neo-Nazi activity throughout Europe.

5. *N S Bulletin* (1974–1983) and

6. *White Power* (1969–1978): both periodicals are published by the National Socialist White People's Party, which changed its name to the New
Order in 1982. This organization is headed by Matt Koehl, with headquar-
ters in Arlington, Virginia, and later New Berlin, Wisconsin. This organization is the direct descendant of the original American neo-Nazi organization,
the American Nazi Party, founded in 1958 by George Lincoln Rockwell.
The New Order has attempted to form a National Socialist community,
called "Nordland," in Wisconsin. According to the ADL,

> the New Order is more than just the oldest neo-Nazi group in the
> U.S.; it is also the most stable and is ahead of others in organization,
> discipline, and experience . . . it has sought to adapt its "Aryan" doc-
> trines somewhat, emphasizing white racism as much as anti-Semitism.
> Still, the New Order is the most direct descendant of Hitler's party
> among the neo-Nazi groups. (Anti-Defamation League 1988a, 50)

Koehl has also led the World Union of National Socialists, which provides
international connections among neo-Nazi groups.

7. *NSV Report* (1983–1993): quarterly newsletter of the National Socialist Vanguard, started in 1983, and headed by neo-Nazis Rick Cooper and
Dan Stewart, former National Socialist White People's Party members. This

group has closely aligned itself with the Church of Jesus Christ Christian Aryan Nations, a Christian Identity church, in Coeur d'Alene, Idaho. Cooper has declared, "I am in this movement for life and I am willing to risk exposure, ridicule and various types of harassment for my beliefs and actions" (Anti-Defamation League 1988b, 46).

8. *The Thunderbolt* (1974–1984): published by the National States Rights Party (NSRP), founded in 1958, and edited by J. B. Stoner and Edward Fields, "among the most extreme anti-black, anti-Semitic hatemongers in the U.S." (Anti-Defamation League 1988a, 29). The ADL describes the NSRP as "ideologically hybrid . . . a bridge between the Ku Klux Klan and the American Nazi groups. *The Thunderbolt* had long been the most widely read publication among the Klans and other hate groups" (Anti-Defamation League 1988a, 44). Problems began for the organization in 1983, when Stoner, party chair, was jailed for conspiracy involving the bombing of a black church in 1958. In the 1960s, the NSRP was considered "the most militant organized foe" of the civil rights movement (Anti-Defamation League 1988a, 159). Stoner was a political candidate for numerous offices in Georgia throughout the 1970s, including a run for lieutenant governor in 1974, which garnered him 71,000 votes, over 10 percent of the votes cast for twelve different candidates. By 1987 the NSRP dissolved. Fields continued publishing *The Thunderbolt*, but the publication faced financial ruin.

9. *The Torch* (1977–1979): published by the White People's Committee to Restore God's Laws, a division of the Church of Jesus Christ, a Christian Identity church, and

10. *White Patriot* (1979–1984): newsletter of the Knights of the Ku Klux Klan, the second largest Klan group, are both edited by Thomas Robb. Robb is national KKK "chaplain" as well as minister of the Church of Jesus Christ, a Christian Identity church in Arkansas. Robb has close ties to David Duke's National Association for the Advancement of White People, as well as with neo-Nazis in the United States and West Germany. According to Klanwatch, "Identity Church movement promotes an extreme racist ideology based on the belief that the survival of the white race depends on purging the U.S. of minorities or exterminating them in a worldwide race war" (Klanwatch Intelligence Report 1991, 3).

MISCELLANEOUS ISSUES

The Stimely collection contained sporadic issues of the following periodicals. While I was unable to review these publications over an extended period of time, I chose to include them in order to ensure that I surveyed as wide a range of publications as possible in my research.

11. *Crusader* (no dates): subtitled "the voice of the white majority," the *Crusader* is published by the Knights of the Ku Klux Klan, led at that time by Grand Wizard David Duke, out of Metairie, Louisiana. While the newsletters contain no dates, the issues I reviewed were published in the 1970s.

12. *The Fiery Cross* (1979): published in Swartz, Louisiana, this is the official organ of The United Klans of America (UKA), headed by Imperial Wizard Robert Shelton, in Tuscaloosa, Alabama. Founded in 1960, UKA was the largest Klan organization of the 1960s and 1970s, with tens of thousands of members. The organization was composed of smaller Klan organizations throughout the South. In 1979, twenty members were indicted and thirteen found guilty in connection with violent racist acts in Alabama, and in 1985 five members were arrested and two pleaded guilty to planning and training for terrorist acts against minorities. This organization is now defunct as a result of a 1987 civil trial which awarded seven million dollars in damages to the family of an African American teen killed in 1981.

13. *The National Socialist* (1982–1983): published by The World Union of National Socialists, established by George Lincoln Rockwell, to provide connections among neo-Nazi organizations throughout the world. This organization was later headed by Matt Koehl, leader of the National Socialist White People's Party.

14. *The Northlander* (1978): no information on this publication has been located; neither the Southern Poverty Law Center nor the Anti-Defamation League, both organizations that track white supremacist organizations and their publications, have information on this publication.

15. *N S KAMPFRUF/ N S Mobilizer* (1974–1983): published by the National Socialist League, founded in January 1974 and directed by Russel R. Veh. The National Socialist League is a homosexual, male, neo-Nazi group with a small membership, founded by former members of the National Socialist White People's Party. This publication's name was later changed to *Race and Reason* (Anti-Defamation League 1988a, 46).

16. *The Spotlight* (1986): published by the Liberty Lobby, the most active anti-Semitic organization in the United States, founded in 1957 and lead by Willis A. Carto. Carto is also a founder of the revisionist Institute for Historical Review. Publication of *The Spotlight* peaked in 1981 at 300,000, and was down to 104,000 in 1987. While the Southern Poverty Law Center classifies this organization as anti-Semitic but not white su-

premacist, *The Spotlight* has featured favorable profiles of David Duke, for-mer Klan leader and founder of the National Association for the Advancement of White People, as well as favorable coverage of the white supremacist movement.

17. *Voice of German Americans* (1977–1980): no information has been located on this publication. Neither the Southern Poverty Law Center nor the Anti-Defamation League have information on this periodical.

18. *The Western Guardian* (1980): published by Western Guard America, out of Roanoke, Virginia. This Christian Identity periodical began publication in 1980. "Western Guard America's primary purpose is to get out as much racialist-oriented literature to as many White people as possi-ble" (*Western Guardian*, vol.1, no.1 [April 1980], 1). This organization does not maintain a membership but distributes this periodical to white suprema-cists across the spectrum of organizations.

19. I included one novel, *The Turner Diaries,* in my data because I found that it was frequently cited, advertised, quoted, and referred to throughout the publications I reviewed. It is considered the "manifesto of the white underground" (Ridgeway 1990, 65), and deals specifically with issues of cen-tral concern to this research. Published in 1978, *The Turner Diaries* was written by Andrew Macdonald, the pseudonym of William Pierce. Pierce is the one-time leader of the American Nazi Party and founder and leader of the National Alliance. Called "a Handbook for White Victory," *The Turner Diaries* was initially published in installments in the *National Vanguard*. Widely read and distributed, and considered essential reading by a wide range of white supremacist organizations, *The Turner Diaries* "fantasizes about the overthrow of the American government by superpatriots who kill Jews and non-whites, destroy Israel, and establish an 'Aryan' nation and world" (Anti-Defamation League 1988a, 40). This book has been so influ-ential that National Alliance member Robert Mathews founded and mod-eled The Order after the terrorist organization in *The Turner Diaries*. The Order "attempted revolution against the U.S. Government [which] resulted in a spree of criminal violence in 1983 and 1984, including armed robberies which netted more than $4 million" and the murder of Denver radio talk show host Alan Berg (Anti-Defamation League 1988a, 40). The Oklahoma City bombing appears to have been modeled after incidents in the novel.

INDEX

ABOUT THE AUTHOR

Abby L. Ferber received her Ph.D. from the University of Oregon. She is an assistant professor of sociology at the University of Colorado at Colorado Springs where she teaches courses on race, gender, and social theory.